Praise for the Book

"This is AI explained in the most lucid way, with no jargon. It encourages and empowers you to decide how to incorporate this new superpower into your life and work."
– **Rama Bijapurkar, author and thought leader on business and consumer strategy**

"AI will change our world forever. To thrive in this new age, we must embrace it and become AI-literate. This book is the best way to do that – read it to become irreplaceable."
– **C.P. Gurnani, Founder, AIonOS; former CEO and Managing Director, Tech Mahindra**

"AI is transforming everything – including how and what we learn. Becoming AI-literate is no longer optional, and this is the book to read if you want to get there."
– **Pramath Raj Sinha, Chairman, Ashoka University**

"As someone deeply immersed in making AI accessible, I'm impressed by how this book transforms AI literacy from an abstract concept into a concrete, sequential journey. It offers something genuinely new in the crowded AI space – a structured framework that grows with the reader. This isn't just another technical manual or philosophical exploration, but a hands-on guide that recognizes AI literacy as a new business essential. Jaspreet Bindra and Anuj

Magazine have created something uniquely valuable for anyone looking to move beyond surface-level AI interactions and truly harness its transformative potential."
– Sudarshan Kamath, Founder, smallest.ai

"Jaspreet and Anuj demystify the complexities of artificial intelligence, empowering readers with the knowledge to navigate and leverage AI technologies in their personal and professional lives. This insightful guide is essential for anyone looking to become AI-literate."
– Sanjiv Mehta, Executive Chairman, L Catterton India; former Chair and CEO, Hindustan Unilever

"It is rare to find a book that explains AI simply or shows you how to use it practically in your day-to-day work. This book manages to do both."
– Bev Burgess, Co-Founder and CEO, Inflexion Group, UK

YOUR GUIDE TO AI LITERACY

Jaspreet Bindra and Anuj Magazine

🌀 juggernaut

JUGGERNAUT BOOKS
C-I-128, First Floor, Sangam Vihar, Near Holi Chowk,
New Delhi 110080, India

First published by Juggernaut Books 2025

Copyright © Jaspreet Bindra and Anuj Magazine 2025

10 9 8 7 6 5

P-ISBN: 9789353452339
E-ISBN: 9789353453534

The views and opinions expressed in this book are the author's own. The facts contained herein were reported to be true as on the date of publication by the author to the publishers of the book, and the publishers are not in any way liable for their accuracy or veracity.

All rights reserved. No part of this publication may be reproduced, transmitted, or stored in a retrieval system in any form or by any means without the written permission of the publisher.

Typeset in Adobe Caslon Pro by R. Ajith Kumar, Noida

Printed at Thomson Press India Private Limited

> *"The real question is not whether machines think but whether men do."*
>
> — B.F. SKINNER

Contents

1. Introduction: The Age of AI Literacy   1
2. Demystifying AI   14
3. AI, Work and Jobs   36
4. The Future of AI and the Need for Literacy   53
5. Building Your AI Literacy   69
6. Foundational AI Literacy: READS   83
7. Intermediate AI Literacy: WRITES   127
8. Advanced AI Literacy: ADDS   170
9. Strategic AI Literacy: THINKS   206
10. Agentic AI Literacy: DOES   262

A Continuation   295
Acknowledgements   301
A Note on the Authors   304

1

Introduction

The Age of AI Literacy

"A year spent in artificial intelligence is enough to make one believe in God."

— ALAN PERLIS

Since human beings learnt to read, write, add and multiply, these skills have distinguished the knowledgeable from the ignorant, the rich from the poor, and the literate from the illiterate. Countries and societies have been measured not just on how healthy and wealthy their people are, but also on their level of literacy and education. Literacy has been a key indicator of human development and other indices that routinely differentiate developed countries from the underdeveloped, and the rich from the poor. While the definition of literacy varies from country to country and keeps evolving, it usually refers to proficiency in reading, writing and simple arithmetic – namely addition, subtraction, multiplication and division.

In the brave new age of AI, we believe that this definition will see a radical shift, encompassing not only reading, writing and arithmetic, but also *knowing how to work naturally and innately with generative AI (GenAI)*. As AI rapidly diffuses into our work, education, business, society and day-to-day life, it will be critical to learn how to operate AI tools like ChatGPT, Perplexity, Copilot and others in order to streamline both our professional and personal lives. As AI agents become coworkers, collaborators and even enter our family spaces, it will be important to treat AI as another common language that allows for efficacy in all spheres of life. If and when AGI becomes available, coexistence with AI will be inevitable, making AI literacy essential.

What is AI Literacy?

It must be pointed out that literacy is different from training, or upskilling, or even expertise. Literacy involves learning a language – its patterns, structures and grammar. Once you understand it, you can use it to read a story, write a poem or make sense of your bills. What literacy doesn't involve is learning to author essays or gaining expertise in algebra. One can acquire these skills only upon developing an understanding of a language's fundamental rules and structures; after this, we can "upskill" ourselves to any higher level of linguistic or mathematical expertise that we desire. But, if we are not literate to begin with, it means

Introduction

we do not have the basics or the fundamentals required to progress to higher-order functioning. Linguistic and mathematical literacy were essential for us to become educated, employed and successful; in the same way, AI literacy will be just as critical in the years to come.

Over the past many years, we, the authors of this book, have had the privilege of engaging with AI in numerous capacities – working with it in enterprises, leveraging it as a catalyst for digital transformation, delivering keynote addresses at global forums, providing advisory and consulting services to organizations on their AI roadmaps and writing extensively on the subject in leading publications. Through these diverse experiences, one key insight has consistently stood out: while AI is undeniably one of the most transformative forces of our time, a significant knowledge gap persists in understanding how to effectively harness its potential. This gap continues to become larger, as AI develops at the speed of silicon, with new innovations and models being released almost on a daily basis. Almost everyone we met during the process has been searching for a way to become more knowledgeable about these most fundamental technologies of our time. We believe that every single one of them needs to start by becoming AI-literate. This book is our effort to make it possible, thereby democratizing AI literacy and ensuring that both individuals and organizations can confidently engage with and benefit from AI.

To realize this vision, we created and launched AI&Beyond (www.aiandbeyond.ai), a company with the mission to "Build AI Literacy in Organisations. And Beyond." Since then, we have organized numerous AI Literacy Bootcamps – three-hour to day-long experiential workshops which enable participants to experience and learn the plethora of AI tools at our disposal, and how to use some of them to solve their own business problems, as well as boost their own and their teams' productivity and creativity. It has been heartening to see them start to use these tools as their "second brains" and an "extra pair of hands" almost immediately upon realizing the expansive power of AI. These sessions have helped professionals from diverse backgrounds – marketers, educators, lawyers, business leaders, even students – integrate AI into their workflows, enhancing their efficiency, creativity and decision-making capabilities. Witnessing the transformative impact of AI on these participants reinforced our belief that AI literacy is not a luxury; it is indeed a necessity.

Why Become AI Literate?

We believe that AI can become a democratized technology, and become available to everyone – irrespective of income, education and nationality. The miracle of GenAI is its sheer accessibility; anyone with a smart phone or a PC with an internet connection can access it free of cost.

Introduction

As Mary Mesaglio of Gartner says: "GenAI is not just a technology or just a business trend. It is a profound shift in how humans and machines interact."[1] When you write a prompt on ChatGPT, you are actually "writing code", using your natural language to make a machine do something. Earlier, this required years of software engineering training; now one can achieve it by being literate in one's natural language and using it effectively through their chosen AI tool. While we will still need specialized and advanced education and training for software engineers and other IT professionals to build and work on advanced AI, basic AI literacy needs to extend beyond computer science and reach professionals across industries. The democratization of AI knowledge can help individuals across different business sectors and social strata leverage AI to improve efficiency, productivity, innovation and ultimately their quality of life. AI-powered tutors, personalized learning systems and automated grading mechanisms are revolutionizing the way students acquire knowledge. This shift necessitates that both educators and learners embrace AI literacy to maximize its benefits. A teacher equipped with AI tools can provide more personaliszed guidance, just as a student familiar with AI applications can accelerate their learning process. The broader the reach of AI literacy, the greater the collective progress within society.

---

[1] "Gartner Says AI Ambition and AI-Ready Scenarios Must Be a Top Priority for CIOs for next 12-24 Months." Gartner. 6 November 2023. https://tinyurl.com/3frcfzkk.

Will AI Take Our Jobs?

One of the most significant concerns surrounding AI is, of course, its impact on jobs. Every technological revolution brings disruption, and AI is no exception. While it is true that AI and automation will render some jobs obsolete, it is equally true that they will create new opportunities. The key to thriving in this era of rapid technological advancement is not to resist change but to adapt to it. Understanding AI, learning how to work alongside it and utilizing it to enhance one's capabilities will be the defining factors of success in the years to come. Thus, if you are a software engineer, knowing how to work with AI tools like GitHub, Copilot and Cursor will make you much better at your job; a marketer working with NotebookLM or Copy.ai will be more creative and efficient than their AI-ignorant colleagues; a lawyer working with Harvey will be more proficient; and the list goes on. The AI-supercharged professional will be able to do the job of three of her colleagues. As we have been saying ad infinitum, *it is not AI that will take your job, but someone using AI who will*. So, it is incumbent on you to learn how to work with AI and remain relevant for this new era – to become the replacer, rather than the "replacee"!

Introduction

How to Read this Book

We start this book with Chapter 2, demystifying the technology and philosophy of Artificial Intelligence – what is it, where it came from and why it is so important and fundamental. There is an abundance of information on AI as it moves at blitz speed every day, and it becomes increasingly difficult to keep up with it or even understand what it is. So, we cut through the clutter to make you understand its fundamentals and impact in simple terms.

Next, in Chapter 3, we spell out why AI is important for your work, and what jobs it will augment, create and destroy. Here we address people's biggest apprehension around AI: Is AI a job killer? Will my children find jobs in the AI era? We tackle these question head on and provide insight into the effect of AI in the job market and what we could do to survive and thrive in the professional world.

In Chapter 4, we explain how and where AI is moving and what we can expect it to revolutionize in our life, businesses and the world at large. This chapter will, hopefully, help you understand why there is no option but to be AI-literate to better navigate the future.

It is in Chapter 5 that we come to the core of the book – 'Building Your AI Literacy'. This chapter has simple and intuitive frameworks on how to achieve this literacy step by step, eventually becoming proficient and fluent in AI. The simple visual frameworks act as stepping stones in the succeeding chapters, for gradual yet steady progress in this literacy exercise.

The later chapters (from Chapters 6 to 10) are structured around the core components of AI literacy, which we have categorized along the basic tenets of literacy itself: READS, WRITES and ADDS. After this, we go beyond literacy to fluency and proficiency with THINKS and DOES. The first three represent the foundations of traditional literacy – reading, writing and arithmetic. The next two explore our cognitive ability of thinking, and our power to act on our thoughts. These five pillars encapsulate the essential ways in which AI interacts with the world and, consequently, how we should interact with AI.

1. READS refers to AI's ability to process and interpret text, audio and visual data and so how it can help you summarize content to read faster, or translate languages, or even conduct advanced research on topics you want to know more about. We have tried to make this super simple by capturing five skills that AI can enhance for you; these skills correspond with the letters R, E, A, D and S, making them easy to remember: Real-time Language Access; Edit and Enhance Content; Advanced AI Search and Research; Document Summarization; and using AI as a Sparring Partner.
2. WRITES explores AI's role in content creation, from drafting emails and reports to generating marketing copies and even creative writing. With WRITES, AI

can help you Write Documents; for Reach, Branding, Marketing; Images and Video Creation; Tailored Communication and Presentations; Email and Messaging; and to Speak and Collaborate with AI to write better stuff.
3. ADDS covers AI's analytical and problem-solving abilities to enhance and augment human work by analysing information, automate certain processes and decode reams of data, to improve your efficiency and decision-making. In the ADDS ability, AI can help you Automate Core Processes; Decode Markets and Competition; practise Data Driven Decision Making; and Sentiment Analysis.
4. THINKS is where AI truly comes into its own and becomes even more human-like by becoming our thought partner to help us leverage it for strategy, brainstorming and planning. THINKS is all about Thought Leadership; Human Resources and Human-Agent Optimization; Innovation and Brainstorming; New Product Development; Knowledge Management and using AI as a Second Brain; and Strategic Planning and Foresight.
5. DOES focuses on the action and automation capabilities of AI agents, streamlining repetitive tasks and enabling us to focus on higher-order thinking. DOES covers Delegating to AI Agents; Orchestrate Complex Processes; Execute and Expedite; and manage Support and Customer Success.

The final chapter of the book, Chapter 11, is not a conclusion, but actually the start of your journey towards co-existing with AI. Much like learning a language, AI literacy is a journey of continuous learning. As a child progresses from reading the alphabet, to short stories, to complex novels and research papers, so will you progress in your AI journey. Many of the AI tools we have explained and used in the book will endure, but many will be continuously updated, and even more new tools will be created. While the book was written at a certain point in time, it will effectively build your AI literacy and, hopefully, the curiosity and drive to continuously learn more. In that spirit, our last chapter is a continuation rather than a conclusion.

Each section of this book is designed to not only explain these concepts but also provide actionable insights, practical tools, guidance on writing the right prompts, best practices and strategies for minimizing data leaks through real-world case studies that demonstrate how AI can be integrated into professional and personal workflows.

While the book has been written in a continuous and logical flow from Chapter 1 to 11, it has been designed such that you can specifically pick and choose what you would like to read and learn on a particular day, based on your personal and work needs. Chapters 2–4 give you the history of AI, demystifying it and explaining how it will impact work and our jobs and speculate about the future of AI. If you are curious about all of that, we suggest you read these chapters continuously. Chapter 5, as pointed out earlier, is the pivotal chapter which kickstarts your learning journey to become AI-literate. We recommend reading this chapter before you dive into the core Chapters 6–10. After that, you can decide the order in which you'd prefer to read, depending on what you want to learn. In fact, you can even pick some of the core skills within each chapter. If you are a strategy professional, for example, Chapter 9 – with its THINKS framework – will be highly relevant. If you are a marketer or creative professional, you would perhaps prefer Chapter 7 and its WRITES framework. Reading the entire book from start to finish, in whatever order, will make you 100 per cent AI-literate.

Writing this book has been an exercise in practising what we preach, or "eating our own dogfood", as they say in the technology world, where both of us come from. We have leveraged AI tools at various stages of its creation, from research and outlining to drafting and refining content, and have transparently informed the reader of which tools were used and where. This experience has underscored one of the key messages of this book: AI is not here to replace human intelligence but to augment it. The speed, efficiency and insights that AI offers have allowed us to produce a more comprehensive and well-structured book in a fraction of the time it would have otherwise taken. In fact, this has made us think of AI not only as artificial intelligence, but as augmented intelligence.

This book is not just about understanding AI; it is about applying AI in meaningful ways. Whether you are a corporate professional looking to streamline your workflow, an entrepreneur seeking to scale your business, a student preparing for the future job market or simply someone curious about how AI can enhance everyday life, this book will provide you with the tools and knowledge to become literate and fluent in AI, and to navigate the AI-driven world with confidence.

AI is often perceived as a complex, intimidating subject. Our goal with this book is to make AI literacy approachable, engaging and practical. We want readers to walk away not just with theoretical knowledge but with hands-on skills that they can immediately apply in their personal and professional lives.

As you embark on this journey through the pages of this book, we encourage you to experiment with the AI tools explained here, challenge yourself to think differently and explore new ways in which AI can enhance your work and life. The future belongs to those who can adapt, learn and innovate – and AI literacy is the foundation upon which this future will be built. AI is not just a tool; it is a culture and a mindset. As we say later in the book, "Invite AI to the table every time." The more we integrate AI into our daily lives, the more we unlock new ways to be efficient, creative and forward-thinking. The world is moving rapidly, and those who can effectively collaborate with AI will have

Introduction

a distinct advantage going forward. This book will serve as your guide to navigating this fast-evolving world.

We hope these pages serve as a valuable resource in your AI literacy journey and empower you to harness the full potential of artificial intelligence. Let us go beyond fear and uncertainty and step into a world of infinite possibilities. AI is not just shaping the future; it is shaping the present. The question is: are you ready to make the most of it?

This chapter was written with the help of ChatGPT 4o Canvas.

2

Demystifying AI

"By far, the greatest danger of Artificial Intelligence is that people conclude too early that they understand it."
— ELIEZER YUDKOWSKY

Before we go deeper into AI, let us talk about us, its creator — humans. A key reason why humans became the apex species is our ability to create tools and use them well; sometimes we call these tools, technologies. A set of technologies we created powered the Agricultural Revolution, which made food accessible and plentiful. Another set of technologies led to the Industrial Revolution, which democratized labour. The Internet search and the World Wide Web made information free. Inevitably, at the dawn of each revolution, we were both excited and frightened by what the future might bring. Today, we stand at the cusp of another revolution, where intelligence becomes free and accessible to everyone. This revolution is propelled largely by a technology we call artificial intelligence. Again,

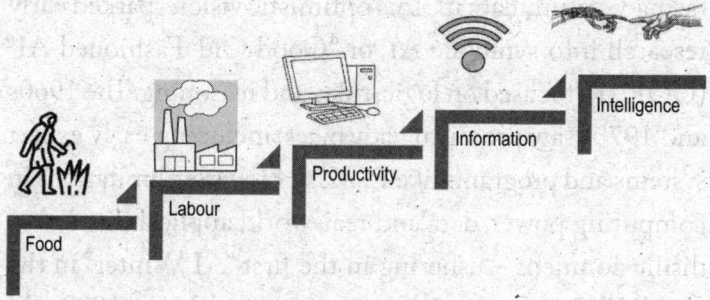

Revolutions in Human History

understandably, as we enter the dawn of this revolution, we are filled with conflicting emotions of fear and excitement.

The History of AI

The history of AI, on the other hand, can be described as a tale of three papers. The first of these papers[1] was published in 1955–56 at the famous Dartmouth Conference where the so-called fathers of AI – Marvin Minsky, John McCarthy and Claude Shannon – first coined the term "artificial intelligence". The paper proposed that "every aspect of learning or any other feature of intelligence can in principle be so precisely described that a machine can

---

[1] McCarthy, John, Marvin L Minsky, Nathaniel Rochester, and Claude E Shannon. 1955. "A Proposal for the Dartmouth Summer Research Project on Artificial Intelligence, August 31, 1955." AI Magazine 27 (4): 12–12. https://doi.org/10.1609/aimag.v27i4.1904.

be made to simulate it. This optimistic vision sparked early research into symbolic AI, or "Good Old-Fashioned AI" (GOFAI), focused on logic, rules and reasoning. The 1960s and 1970s saw promising advances, including early expert systems and programs like ELIZA. However, limitations in computing power, data and real-world applicability led to disillusionment – ushering in the first "AI Winter" in the mid-1970s, as funding and interest waned. In the 1980s, AI experienced a resurgence with expert systems like XCON to configure computer systems or MYCIN for medical diagnosis, which started getting adopted by businesses. But once again, scalability and brittleness became issues, leading to another downturn in the early 1990s. Still, this period wasn't stagnant: foundational progress in machine learning, probabilistic models and neural networks quietly continued. The 2000s brought a shift – better hardware, large datasets and open-source software fuelled the rise of machine learning. Algorithms like support vector machines and decision trees found real-world applications in search, recommendation and fraud detection. A turning point came in 2012 when a deep convolutional neural network – AlexNet – won the ImageNet competition, dramatically outperforming others in image recognition. This revived interest in deep learning, leading to breakthroughs in vision, speech and language. This pre-GenAI is called analytical AI or discriminative AI by most experts.

The Creation of GenAI

The second paper[2] came out in 2017 in the labs of Google Brain. Google Brain was a pioneering deep learning research team at Google, founded in 2011 by AI legends Andrew Ng, Jeff Dean and Greg Corrado. It began as a Google X project and gained fame for training neural networks to recognize cats in YouTube videos without supervision. Google Brain played a key role in advancing deep learning and helped integrate AI across Google products like Search, Translate and Photos. It also contributed to the development of TensorFlow, an open-source machine learning framework, and published influential research in areas like computer vision, natural language processing and reinforcement learning. However, it was this landmark paper, titled "Attention Is All You Need", which proposed a new kind of algorithm called the Transformer. The transformer is the T of GPT, which stands for Generative Pre-trained Transformer. Google scientists built on the architecture proposed on the paper and created this new kind of algorithm. The transformer created early GenAI models like BERT by Google, but

---

[2] Vaswani, Ashish, Noam Shazeer, Niki Parmar, Jakob Uszkoreit, Llion Jones, Aidan N. Gomez, Łukasz Kaiser, and Illia Polosukhin. 2017. "Attention Is All You Need." Advances in Neural Information Processing Systems 30 (4): 5998–6008.

the real breakthrough happened when a then small AI research lab called OpenAI took this and started creating the GPT series of GenAI models, culminating in GPT 3.5, or what we call ChatGPT. OpenAI was a pioneering AI research lab created in 2015, with a mission to "advance digital intelligence in a way that would benefit humanity as a whole", and thus create AGI or artificial general intelligence. The founders, including Elon Musk, Sam Altman, Ilya Sutskever and others, aimed to ensure that AI would be developed and used in a manner that was safe and beneficial for mankind. Initially, OpenAI was established as a non-profit organization, which allowed it to focus on research without the pressure of generating financial returns. Their efforts towards taking the transformer to create ChatGPT popularized what we now call GenAI; it pulled AI out of the background and placed it front and centre.

The third paper,[3] which was published as recently as January 2025, was concurrent with the release of a Chinese model called DeepSeek R1. This paper forever changed the narrative of AI, as we will see later in the chapter.

---

[3] "GitHub - Deepseek-Ai/DeepSeek-R1." 2025. GitHub. https://tinyurl.com/yc2ws578.

Demystifying AI

 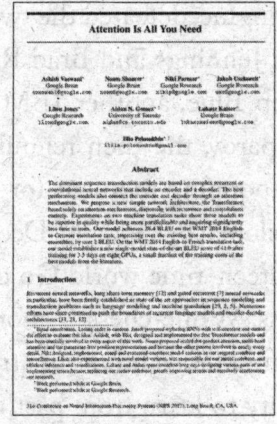

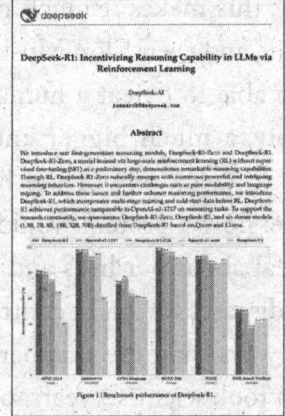

A Tale of Three Papers

Analytical AI

While the first paper defining AI came out in 1955, AI first entered popular consciousness firmly in 2011 with the much-publicized episode of *Jeopardy*, where Watson, IBM's

AI engine, defeated the two reigning human champions – Ken Jennings and Brad Rutter. Fifteen years before this, Deep Blue, another IBM computer, had defeated Gary Kasparov, the then reigning chess world champion. The eye-popping moment for AI was when AlphaGo, an AI developed by Google's DeepMind, defeated Lee Sedol, the eighteen-time world Go champion. Go is different from chess. While chess is more deterministic, Go requires a deep understanding of strategy, acute judgement and an ability to learn from past moves – classically very human traits. Supposedly, this makes it much more difficult for machines to master, and even Elon Musk thought that an AI would only be able to defeat a human Go champion by 2026. Arguably, a much bigger and celebrated AI achievement was to crack one of the hardest problems in medical science: how a protein would fold. This event decides a great deal about our lives and health, from our physiology to the diseases we might contract. But a protein can fold in more ways than the number of atoms in the known universe. It took scientists years to correctly predict how a protein might fold using X-ray crystallography and other techniques. By comparison, DeepMind's AlphaFold used Deep Learning to figure out the folding possibilities of hundreds of millions of proteins, reducing years of work to just weeks.

Beyond these near miracles, AI has been powering large swathes of industry as well as our lives for decades now. The recommendation engines built into Netflix and Amazon telling you what to watch or buy are powered by AI. So are social networks serving up reels and videos to you, personalized for your taste on Instagram, TikTok and YouTube. The fact that you can almost always find an Uber nearby is thanks to the routing algorithms that AI power; even Google Maps is underpinned by AP and so are deliveries. Behind the scenes, AI predicts when a machine will fail so that it can be repaired beforehand, AI-driven robots manage warehouses and supply chains powered by AI perform optimization and routing calculations at blinding speed. The financial sector is a huge user of AI when it comes to algorithmic trading, personalized stock recommendations and pricing algorithms. The hyper-targeted Google and Facebook ads have long been perfected by AI, as are the data centres which enable and host AI in the first place.

The ultimate manifestation of AI is the driverless car, which uses computer vision as well as machine learning and deep learning to navigate by itself. We are yet to fully achieve autonomous driving, but the near-autonomous experience now offered by Cruise, Waymo and Tesla is also courtesy of AI. Smart metering – real-time information on energy usage, helping to reduce bills; more efficient grid operation and storage; predictive infrastructure maintenance – is one of the use cases of AI in energy. Healthcare is another heavy AI user with regards to personalized medicine, robotic surgeries and the more mundane tasks of patient scheduling and triaging. So is education, with EdTech players serving up personalized content and mentoring to students, working towards the dream of a personalized tutor for every child on the planet.

GenAI

All of the above were working to remake our lives mostly for the better even before the second paper "Attention Is All You Need" brought in the transformer, leading to GenAI, and the eventual launch of ChatGPT on 30 November 2022. OpenAI's ChatGPT is what brought AI out of the hands of the data scientists and AI engineers and placed it in the hands of people like you and me, allowing us to experience the power of this technology first-hand. Within the first five days, it had a million users and raced to a hundred million in two months, the fastest digital app in history. GenAI is the culmination of decades of efforts in neural networks, deep learning and natural language processing, but it is different from the AI that we had been used to so far. Analytical AI was about analysing large sets of data, drawing patterns from it and predicting what could happen with reasonable accuracy. GenAI is different, it is trained on large language datasets of text and images. For example, GPT3 (an ancestor to the powerful GPT and other models today) was trained on all the text available across the entire Internet. In other words, the entire Internet was "downloaded" on a particular day and served as the training date for this transformer model. GPT stands for Generative Pre-Trained Transformer. The T, the transformer, is the revolutionary algorithm which, when fed a set of words, or what we call a prompt can predict the next word or set of words. The P is for pre-training that describes what this model is pre-trained on before being released, which in this case was almost the entire Internet. The G is for generative or the kind of AI that it results in, which generates or creates, rather than analysing or predicting.

GenAI is trained on language. Many thinkers and scientists, Noam Chomsky for example, believe that what separates human beings from other species is not emotion, or intelligence or consciousness, but how we can use language at scale. This efficient and innate use of language allows us to collaborate with eight billion others, making us the earth's most dominant species. More simply put, the powerful transformer algorithms working on this vast mountain of data could predict with astonishing accuracy, speed and scale what the next word would be if you gave it a series of words. These models, tellingly called Large Language Models (LLMs), literally make up stuff as they go along. Since they are probabilistic in nature, rather than deterministic, they are optimized more for believability or plausibility, than the truth or factual information. Thus, they often tend to "hallucinate", though this tendency is diminishing with more powerful models and more advanced ways to tweak the algorithms.

Undeniably, GenAI models are creative: Marc Andreessen, the founder of the storied venture capital firm Andreessen Horowitz or A16Z, was spot on when he said, "If you like what they are saying, they are creative; if you don't, they are hallucinating." There is one more species which makes up stuff as it goes along, is creative and otherwise, and does not know all the facts all the time but can make very convincing arguments. That species is us, human beings. Both GenAI and humans are trained on language, and that is why we get along so well. This is also the reason we tend to anthropomorphize this AI, saying "please" and "thank you" as we would to another human being.

Igniting the AI Revolution

What is undeniable is that ChatGPT ignited the whole AI revolution, dragging us into a new Age of AI at warp speed. OpenAI brought in newer and more powerful models at lightning speed to us over 2023, while 2024 saw other companies arriving on the scene to build "foundation" models – Anthropic released its Claude series, Google developed Gemini and then Gemini 2, Microsoft launched Phi and Orca, Mistral made Mixtral, Meta created LlaMA,

X announced Grok, IBM unleashed WatsonX, to name a few. Thousands of startups and large companies all over the world raced to build applications on top of this amazing new technology – Perplexity for searching, Cursor to write code, Gamma to build presentations, Eleven Labs and Smallest.ai for voice cloning and many more. Microsoft took the lead in infusing AI into all its platforms and productivity software to build Copilots to help us work faster and better, declaring a major pivot and calling itself a Copilot company. Big Tech raced to own this technology – with Amazon, Microsoft, Meta, Google all buying up large equity positions in the hottest AI startups and providing them with much-needed computing power. Lording over all of them is Nvidia, the chip company which raced to become the most valuable company ever, for some time, at $3.5 trillion dollars. Its founder Jensen Huang positioned Nvidia's super powerful GPUs to be the chips that power all of these compute-hungry foundation or frontier models, with more and more powerful models needing ever more Nvidia chips of increasing capability. The AI revolution was truly underway, even as accompanying worries of the ethics involved were hotly debated, with the fear of super intelligence overwhelming human beings looming large, along with the growing concern around how AI was becoming centralized within a few very large tech companies in the US.

DeepSeek R1: Changing the Narrative

The third of the three papers mentioned earlier, published in January 2025, came from an unlikely place: a no-name company called DeepSeek in China. Its DeepSeek R1 foundation model claimed a performance similar to the top-of-the-line GPT-class models, but at a cost less than 10 per cent of what it took to build them. Even more shockingly, it was an open-source model, revealed the paper through its detailed description of DeepSeek's innards. Another surprise was the claim that it was built using older-generation Nvidia chips, and not by a tech company, but by a hedge fund employing fresh AI engineer!

Understandably, the AI world recoiled, with Nvidia's stock dropping like a stone by 17 per cent the day the model came out. While there have been doubts about the cost, DeepSeek has undoubtedly changed the prevailing narrative around AI: that it takes hundreds of millions of dollars to build and needs the latest Nvidia GPUs, requires rare and experienced talent and the efficacy of a large Western tech company. DeepSeek proved that it could be done by smaller companies with lesser amounts of money and without the latest chips. DeepSeek was open to sharing its secret sauce, keeping the tech open source, thereby effectively destabilizing the AI centralization. Since then, newer and more powerful open source models have been spun out of multiple Chinese companies almost on a daily basis, forcing OpenAI and other companies in the US to focus more on reasoning and thinking AI, as well as the quest for AGI.

Defining AI

But what is AI in the first place? AI is not easy to define; it is so vast and general an area that it can mean different things to different people. When John McCarthy coined the term "artificial intelligence" in 1956, he proceeded to define it thus: "Artificial intelligence is the science of making machines do things that would require intelligence if done by people."[4] Kaplan and Haenlein gave a more modern definition, which is more computer science-oriented: "a system's ability to correctly interpret external data, to learn from such data, and to use those learnings to achieve specific goals and tasks through flexible adaptation."[5] The *Oxford English Dictionary* gives a more descriptive and precise definition of AI: "The theory and development of computer systems able to perform tasks normally requiring human intelligence, such as visual perception, speech recognition,

---

[4] Moya, Jose. 2024. "John McCarthy: Pioneer in Artificial Intelligence - Jala University." Jala University. 11 July 2024. https://tinyurl.com/4f74f9cv.

[5] Haenlein, Michael, and Andreas Kaplan. 2019. "A Brief History of Artificial Intelligence: On the Past, Present, and Future of Artificial Intelligence." California Management Review 61 (4): 5–14. https://doi.org/10.1177/0008125619864925.

decision-making, and translation between languages." The definition we like best, however, is the one from the *Encyclopaedia Britannica*, since it brings AI slightly closer to Isaac Asimov's works and science fiction in general: "Artificial intelligence (AI), the ability of a digital computer or computer-controlled robot to perform tasks commonly associated with intelligent beings." Google, Amazon, IBM and Microsoft have their own definitions, which seem to reflect their own visions and businesses better. For example, IBM has started defining AI as augmented intelligence, rather than artificial intelligence, since they believe that AI will "augment human intelligence" rather than replace it. There have been forums where AI has also been called assimilated (or collective) intelligence, since it collects all the data (human and otherwise) in the world and then derives some intelligence from it! AI is sometimes said to also stand for alternative intelligence, since it can be understood as a different kind of intelligence than that humans possess, not unlike octopus intelligence. Kate Crawford famously says in her book *Atlas of AI*[6] that AI is neither artificial (since it requires millions of human "ghost workers" to make it work) nor intelligent (since it is just a pattern reading machine), but that is another story for another book.

---

[6] Kate Crawford. 2021. The Atlas of AI: Power, Politics, and the Planetary Costs of Artificial Intelligence. Yale University Press. ISBN: 9780300264630.

Types and Technologies of AI

Artificial intelligence is an umbrella term for a suite of technologies and terms within it. It is also a bit of a struggle to typify or classify AI, given its vastness and complexity.

One way to segment AI is to classify it as "Weak or Narrow AI" and "Strong or General AI". As the name suggests, Narrow AI focuses on one thing – chess or poker, for example, or voice recognition. Here, every rule and scenario is entered manually, and this is a rules-based, "brute force" AI. Every Narrow AI, in turn, helps to develop a Strong AI. This one is "real" AI, where the machine starts to think, react and perform like a human being. We are yet to arrive at General AI, or AGI, though we are getting closer every year. We also do not have a precise definition for AGI, as the goalposts on what it is move every year.

The main technologies encompassing AI are the following:

- **Machine Learning:** A subset of AI where systems automatically learn patterns and insights from data without explicit instructions. These learned patterns help computers make predictions or decisions on new, unseen data.
- **Supervised Learning:** A type of machine learning where models are trained using labelled datasets, meaning the correct answers or outputs are provided. It enables accurate predictions or classifications on new, unseen data.

- **Unsupervised Learning:** Machine learning where models analyse unlabelled data, discovering inherent structures or patterns without explicit guidance. It's commonly used for clustering, dimensionality reduction and anomaly detection.
- **Deep Learning:** A specialized type of machine learning using layered neural networks to model complex patterns in large volumes of data. It's particularly effective at tasks involving unstructured data like images, speech and text.
- **Natural Language Processing (NLP):** An AI discipline enabling computers to understand, interpret and respond to human languages. It involves tasks such as sentiment analysis, language translation and text summarization.
- **Neural Networks:** Computational architectures inspired by biological neurons, structured in interconnected layers to process information through pattern recognition. They form the backbone of modern AI applications, especially in deep learning.
- **Large Language Models (LLMs):** Sophisticated AI models trained on extensive textual datasets, enabling them to generate coherent, contextually relevant text. They're used for diverse tasks such as writing, summarizing, translating and conversational agents like ChatGPT.

- **GenAI:** AI systems designed specifically to produce original, realistic content – such as text, images, audio or video. It leverages training on extensive datasets to creatively generate novel outputs based on learned patterns.
- **Computer Vision:** An AI field focused on interpreting and analysing visual information from images or video footage. It enables machines to recognize objects, detect events and derive actionable insights similar to human sight.
- **Robotics:** A multidisciplinary field combining engineering, computer science and AI to design, build and operate robots – machines capable of performing tasks autonomously or semi-autonomously. It focuses on creating systems that interact intelligently with the physical world, often handling tasks too dangerous, repetitive or precise for humans.

Key Technical AI Terms

There are other terms and buzzwords you might hear often as you read about GenAI, some of which you will find repeated in the book. Here is a short list of these terms with their definitions:
- **Tokens (in the context of LLMs):** Tokens are units of text (words, characters or sub-words) that language models break sentences into for processing. They form

the basic building blocks for generating or interpreting language.
- **Session:** A specific interaction period between a user and an AI system, where previous inputs and outputs can influence ongoing responses. Sessions help maintain coherent conversations or tasks over multiple interactions.
- **Context Lengths:** The maximum number of tokens an AI model can effectively process or remember in a single interaction. Longer context lengths enable better coherence and recall in ongoing interactions or tasks.
- **Prompts:** User-provided instructions or inputs guiding an AI model's response or output generation. They influence the tone, style, accuracy and relevance of the AI's answers.
- **Transformers:** A neural network architecture that excels in handling sequential data by capturing context through attention mechanisms rather than sequential processing. They are foundational to modern NLP tasks and large language models like GPT.
- **Small Language Models:** Compact, efficient AI language models trained on smaller datasets and computational resources. They offer faster inference and lower cost, suitable for specific, targeted applications.
- **AI Agents:** Autonomous software systems that perceive their environment, make decisions and take actions to achieve specific goals or tasks. They combine

reasoning, decision-making and learning capabilities to function independently or collaboratively in dynamic scenarios.

The Road Ahead

What is undeniable is that AI and GenAI will be as transformative as search, email and social media. Technology continues to evolve, but there are times when something revolutionary happens. One such revolutionary moment was the emergence of the Internet and the World Wide Web (WWW). Email, Search and the Smartphone were other such revolutionary products. They fundamentally changed our lives and businesses; whether for better or worse is up for debate. We believe that GenAI is one such fundamental inflection point. GenAI was not built overnight; it has been many decades in the making, marinating for more than sixty years since the Dartmouth Conference. Perhaps the first LLM was ELIZA, developed by MIT's Joseph Weizenbaum in 1966, as a primitive form of ChatGPT. As we saw, AI has been used in enterprises, social networks, search, logistics and supply chains and almost every other industry for decades; it is like electricity or the steam engine, a GPT, if you like – a General Purpose Technology. Frontier AI companies like OpenAI and DeepMind were created for the express purpose of building AGI, aiming for the famed Singularity, when machine intelligence will match or surpass human intelligence. With the astonishing advances in the last couple of years, that moment may not be far away. As we wrote in the beginning of the chapter, humans are looking at this development with a mixture of excitement and fear.

The fear comes from the very real ethical issues surrounding AI. Privacy and deepfakes are a real concern, as they enable the creation of pornography, fraudulent voices and images and realistic videos at a speed and scale not seen before. These threaten to violate personal privacy, endanger human rights and even subvert democracy. The legions of deepfakes generated before the US and Indian elections were a testament to this, and the millions of dollars of fraud committed using voice and video deepfakes are becoming a significant menace. Privacy violations using surveillance systems driven by AI are threatening to upend society.

AI is also known to damage the environment and accelerate global warming: the massive LLMs require vast amounts of energy to be trained, the data centres where AI lives emit copious amounts of CO_2 and the GPU and chip fabs suck enormous amounts of water from already depleted resources. AI models are also biased, in the same way and sometimes more than humans are, serving up politically and racially biased answers, images and videos to prompts. There is also the wide fear of job loss, as AI models become increasingly powerful. While these issues are undeniable, the good news is that countries, corporations and societies are cognizant of this fact. Unlike in social media, where complete laissez faire innovation turned it into a malevolent force more than a force of good, organizations have started creating principles, guidelines and even regulations to contain and guardrail AI. The EU AI Act is one example of this. In our estimation, it is much safer for, say, a child to use ChatGPT than Instagram.

What is inevitable is that we are now squarely in the Age of AI; the technology is here to stay and becoming more capable every day at a furious pace. We will have to learn to live with it, and even better if we learn how to leverage it to become better at our life and work. We believe that more than any other aspect of our life, GenAI will impact how we work and the kind of jobs we do. In the words of the Chinese AI guru Kai Fu Lee: "AI is serendipity. It is here to liberate us from routine jobs, and it is here to remind us what it is that makes us human."

This chapter was written with the help of ChatGPT 4o Canvas, Claude Sonnet 4.7 and Perplexity.ai

3

AI, Work and Jobs

"Those who cannot learn to live with AI will be replaced by those who can."

— MAX TEGMARK

By far, the biggest concern around AI is how it might impact jobs. "Is my job safe?" and "Will my children find jobs in the age of AI?" are common refrains today. This is not surprising, since AI is a cognitive technology, perhaps the first tool we have invented that mimics our brain. Thus, it has abilities and expertise that we consider uniquely human – creativity, art, writing, mathematics and coding. Unlike other technologies of the agricultural and industrial revolution, this one does not threaten to replace blue-collar manual labour, or the jobs "other people" do, but white-collar knowledge work, or the jobs "people like us" do. Thus, it ignites a primal fear of loss of livelihood, relevance and one's place in society.

Claude Shannon, the father of Information Theory and an MIT professor, once grumpily remarked, "I visualize a time when we will be to robots what dogs are to humans, and I'm rooting for the machines." Shannon did not seem to like human beings too much, but this quote does lend credence to the same fears and questions that have resurfaced today.

These questions are certainly not being asked for the first time. Every time a revolutionary new technology is unleashed, the same thought fearfully raises its head. It bothered Ned Ludd in 1779 when the spinning jenny was invented, as it threatened to take his job as a textile factory apprentice. He went and smashed a machine or two, catalysing a campaign against textile technology, and started the Luddite movement. New-age Luddites worried about PCs and their job-destroying potential; this movement was particularly strident in India with computers being smashed by workers' unions. We were apprehensive that computers would replace accountants, clerks, secretaries, teachers, consultants and scores of others "like us". The reality, as it turned out, was quite different: the PC and the Internet did destroy a few jobs, but created millions more, and today we cannot imagine our life without them; the IT revolution not only created new jobs, but also catapulted India into a tech superpower.

On that note, let us clarify something: "work" is different from "jobs". Work is generally defined as any effort or activity, physical or mental, undertaken to achieve a result or fulfil a purpose. It encompasses tasks performed for personal satisfaction, family responsibilities, volunteer activities, creative pursuits or professional outcomes. Work can be informal, unpaid and self-directed, often driven by intrinsic motivation or broader life goals rather than financial compensation. A job, on the other hand, refers specifically to paid employment, a structured role within an organization or business where an individual is compensated financially for performing defined duties. Jobs typically involve clear expectations, responsibilities, schedules and performance criteria set by an employer, emphasizing extrinsic rewards such as salary, benefits, promotions and career advancement. The key difference between work and jobs lies in their scope and motivation: work is broader, encompassing any meaningful or purposeful effort, while a job is narrower, explicitly tied to employment and financial remuneration.

Let us tackle work first. A report on AI and the future of work by Microsoft WorkLab offers some interesting revelations: More than half (57 per cent) of a corporate employee's typical workday is devoted to communication like emails, meetings, chats and so on.[1] The remaining 43 per cent is put towards actual creative tasks, and even those sometimes involve creating spreadsheets, documents or slides to present in the aforementioned meetings. No wonder that more than two-thirds of workers complained

---

[1] "Work Trend Index | Will AI Fix Work?" 2023. Www.microsoft.com. 9 May 2023. https://tinyurl.com/y5wfvjj4.

that they did not have uninterrupted focused time during their workday. In fact, when we share this statistic with management executives and employees, we are often told this is wrong – the ratio is more like 70/30 or 80/20 in favour of non-creative to creative work. As former corporate citizens who experienced this for more than two decades before turning entrepreneurs, this resonates strongly with us. While entrepreneurs too face many struggles, our level of productivity has ratcheted up several times, unencumbered by countless meetings discussing the same old issues, similar information being presented to different people in different formats and virtually no time to do any deep thinking.

As the GenAI tidal wave sweeps across industries and offices, we strongly believe that it will affect corporate work more than anything else. We often do not consider work an industry – though it is a several trillion dollar one – and confuse work with jobs. We are rightly worried about how AI will impact jobs, but tend to neglect how it will impact work. Let us explain this through the accompanying chart.[2]

This chart neatly deconstructs knowledge work – the kind that most of our readers would be involved in – into three categories. In the first instance, you "Act" as: an accountant, a programmer, a marketer or a journalist.

---

[2] "Reddit – the Heart of the Internet." 2023. Reddit.com. 27 April 2023. https://tinyurl.com/eb69fwcm.

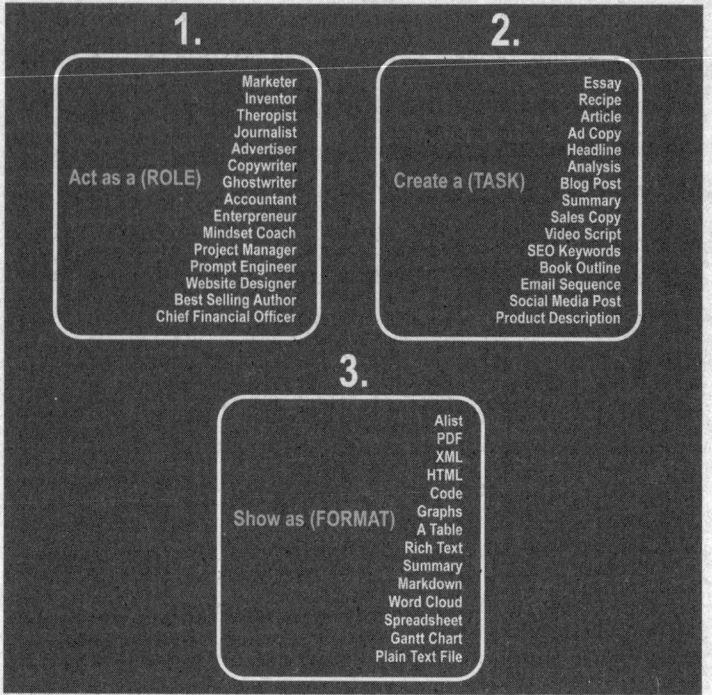

Deconstructing White Collar Work

In the second, you "Show" as a format: a slide, a chart, a spreadsheet, code or a summary. Finally, in the third instance, you "Create" a task: an essay, a recipe, ad copy, code or a sales pitch.

The **show as (Format)** part is probably the most tiresome and repetitive one for a knowledge worker. Good visualization and presentation are important, but very time-consuming and often tedious. This is where GenAI is coming into its own, with innovations like Microsoft

Copilot, Gamma.ai or Napkin.ai building slides, charts and documents on the fly, and even converting content from one format, say a document, to another, say a slide deck. This part, which is the bulk of the 57 per cent non-productive period referred to in the WorkLabs report, will be performed almost entirely by AI, with humans playing a minimal or non-existent role.

The **create a (Task)** part is where humans and AI will work together to co-create. GenAI tools are quite proficient at cognitive tasks and therefore have the potential to help humans in this area of creating or building something. Copy.ai and Jasper.ai help create great marketing material, Stable Diffusion and DALL.E 2 create amazing images for artists and designers, Jukebox helps create ad jingles, and GitHub Copilot or Cursor can collaborate with programmers to write software code. AI will not create the perfect or final pieces of work, at least not yet, and will require a human worker to finesse and fine-tune it to perfection. Take this book, for example: we have worked along with multiple AI tools to create it, and to bring it to life. Not only has it taken lesser time and effort than it would have without these AI collaborators, but it has also been an enjoyable experience, as we were able to brainstorm with a sparring partner, an intelligent, creative co-author who helped us bring our ideas to fruition efficiently and creatively.

What this has allowed us, and will allow all human

workers, is to focus more on the **act as a (Role)** part of work – being a star investigative journalist, a 10x programmer, a creative marketer, a meticulous accountant or a great author. In a sense, it will allow us to go back to the roots of work and spend our hours far more productively doing either high cognitive or intense manual jobs, leaving the mundane and the repetitive ones to AI. While AI can help a marketer create a killer go-to-market strategy presentation, for example, it will not be able to go up in front of the board and deliver it in a persuasive way. It will not be able to make eye contact, read the room for conflicts and agreement, press the hot buttons of the MD and the Chairperson and react and adapt on the fly as needed. It will not be able to inject humour at appropriate moments, or emotion at others, or even capitalize on trust built up over years of experience and camaraderie. When we go deliver keynotes and bootcamps, almost everything we say and show can be accessed through ChatGPT or Claude or Perplexity or even Google Search. However, the audience still willingly pays us humans to come before them and deliver our knowledge. Interestingly, they often insist that we do so in person – even a video call sometimes does not qualify as "showing up". Human communication will perhaps always remain essential, something that embodied or physical AI might never be able to replicate. That is why, Microsoft calls its AI a Copilot; it is not an Autopilot, as it will not do all your work for you; it will not fly the plane for you. The human being remains firmly in the pilot's seat; AI as a co-pilot *helps* us fly the plane; in other words, do our work much more efficiently, productively and creatively.

So, if AI impacts work, then the million dollar question is: what happens to our jobs – which is, for many, one of the central reasons of our existence? A lot has been written on this subject; there are scores of reports and statistics, and we can choose to believe whichever consultant or global multilateral institution we like on what they think about the impact of AI on our jobs. Kai Fu Lee, the acclaimed AI investor and practitioner, has suggested a terrific way to look at the intersection of AI and jobs. His famous matrix (reproduced below) has optimization-to-strategy on one axis, and no compassion-to-full-compassion on another. Low-compassion jobs (like telesales, customer support, dishwashing, radiologist and even truck driver jobs, etc.) will be the first to go, while high-compassion jobs (CEO, M&A expert, teacher, elderly care worker, etc.) will hold out. There will be AI-only jobs, jobs where AI will support humans, and jobs where humans will assist AI. Finally, some jobs will always require humans to perform them: jobs requiring impactful communication, empathy, compassion, trust, creativity and reasoning. In fact, Lee provides a ready-reckoner list of the ten safest fields: psychiatry, therapy, medical care, AI-related research and engineering (ironically, more AI requires more AI engineers and researchers), fiction writing, teaching,

Winning with AI

criminal law, computer science and engineering, science and management.

The authors' view is that we need to look at AI and jobs in a nuanced way, and we do so below through four lenses:

1. **AI will indeed eliminate some jobs.** Since the Agricultural Revolution, every successful new technology

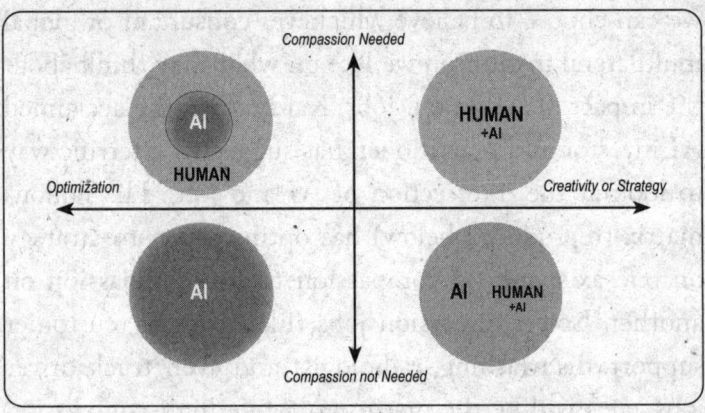

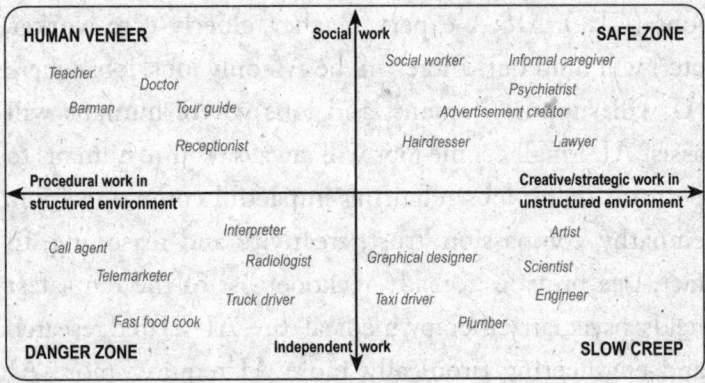

AI and Jobs: The Kai Fu Lee Matrix

invented has supplanted some jobs. The Spinning Jenny of the Industrial Revolution took Ned Ludd's job in the textile mill, the IC engine made horse and buggy drivers obsolete, computers and Microsoft's productivity software meant we did not need typists any more and telephone switchboard operators and lamplighters became a quaint symbol of the past. As per a Goldman Sachs report, this is about 10 per cent of total jobs today.[3] So, if you are a journalist who only summarizes stories into short, digestible bits or an average software programmer who builds payroll software, or even a contact centre agent addressing FAQs from customers, you better start thinking of something else to do! There are many human workers who do these jobs to earn a living – ranging from customer service reps to basic programmers and payroll accountants. As the GenAI express train rolls into organizations, these jobs are increasingly threatened; cases in point are Vodafone, which wants to cut jobs by nearly half and use AI instead, and IBM, which has halted certain kinds of recruitment for the same reason.

2. **There are certain jobs that AI and GenAI won't replace.** Kai Fu Lee has this to say about Moravec's

---

[3] Briggs, Joseph, Jan Hatzius, Devesh Kodnani, and Giovanni Pierdomenico. 2023. "The Potentially Large Effects of Artificial Intelligence on Economic Growth (Briggs/Kodnani)." Goldman Sachs Economic Research. 26 March 2023. https://tinyurl.com/4xkpbrvp.

Paradox: "It is comparatively easy to make computers exhibit adult level performance on intelligence tests, and difficult or impossible to give them the skills of a one-year-old when it comes to perception and mobility."[4] So, an AI like DALL.E 2 might be able to paint like Picasso, but it cannot do what even infants can – such as crawling around, playing with a ball, responding to a mother's smile, feeling affectionate. As Lee wrote, jobs that require human emotions like love or compassion will never be taken over by AI. So, if you are an elderly care worker, a nurse, a construction worker, a farmer or anyone engaged in manual, caring, compassionate work, your job is safe from GenAI. So far, at least. As per the same Goldman Sachs report, this accounts for about 30 per cent of jobs.

3. **AI will create new jobs.** Every single technology since the Agricultural Revolution has created net new jobs, i.e. created more jobs than it has destroyed. At this time, we can't be sure what these new jobs are, and how many there might be. Spinning jennies required operators, the PC created tech jobs of all kinds – so will AI and GenAI. An emerging role is a "prompt engineer". While tinkering with ChatGPT or Claude, you would have noticed that the answer is as good as

---

[4] Lee, Kai-Fu, AI Superpowers: China, Silicon Valley, And The New World Order, HarperCollins, 25 September 2018.

the prompt given, and a prompt engineer will have the skills to write the best prompts, marrying knowledge of language with some domain expertise. Another emerging profession is that of the AI ethicist, with AI's thorny ethical dilemmas spinning out multiple such roles in companies worldwide. Maybe there will be a new kind of role with an expertise in the equivalent of an SEO (Search Engine Optimization) and SEM (Search Engine Marketing) for GenAI. Much like a Search Engine Optimizer works to get search results to favour her clients, and a Search Engine Marketer figures out how your Indian restaurant is ranked higher on Google, these roles will ensure the same when someone asks ChatGPT for its opinion on Indian food. We also see an ORM (Online Reputation Management) for ChatGPT, so that it says good things about you, your restaurant or just Indian food in general.

4. **About 60 per cent of all jobs will be impacted in some way or the other by AI.** Multiple GenAI tools write excellent content and copy, but many times it just hallucinates, since it is optimized for plausibility, not truth. But using AI, a copywriter can generate some initial content ideas for your restaurant very quickly and then refine them. Software programmers are using GitHub Copilot or Claude or Cursor to write code faster. Artists and graphic designers are

using it to brainstorm art ideas for making collateral and visual content. Companies can use it to manage their level one customer service much better, before passing the task on to humans. Translators can use it to turbocharge their translation services, lawyers to scan cases and form initial arguments. The possibilities are endless, and this is where we see AI shine – not by doing your work but making you more creative and productive. A lot of us, especially those who work in creative industries, tend to get threatened by the remarkable creativity that GenAI tools demonstrate. We think that the jobs of artists, writers, authors, journalists, etc. are over, since AI can do all of it so well. The authors disagree; we believe that GenAI is a great creative tool which can actually enhance our creativity. A case in point is Sora, the jaw-dropping text-to-video tool created by OpenAI.[5] Thus, we believe, that the combination of humans and AI is leading us into a new era of creativity. So, if you are a software engineer using GenAI, you could be 2x or 3x better than your colleague who isn't doing so. Ditto for a journalist, marketer, HR manager, or even a CEO.

And so, once again, our core belief bears repeating: it is not AI that will replace you, but a human being using AI.

An interview with Nvidia founder Jensen Huang,

---

[5] "Sora." 2025. https://sora.com/.

brought home to us the most profound effect that AI will have; it will teach us how to be human in the age of AI.[6] In it, Omar Al Olama, the UAE's AI Minister, asks Huang what people should teach themselves and their kids in the age of AI. Huang gives a counterintuitive answer, saying that most people think that we should all learn computer science and AI programming, but we should in fact be doing exactly the opposite. With AI, he says, it is the tech companies' job to create computing technology so that no one has to programme. Instead, everyone in the world becomes a programmer. Thus, the greatest revolution brought about by AI and GenAI is that the gap between human and machine will close completely. In this era, we will engage with computers in human languages like English, Bengali or Spanish and not esoteric ones like C++, Python or PHP, languages of the machines. Both Bill Gates and Satya Nadella of Microsoft echo this. Gates is excited that "AI is the new UI" – the user interface for machines moves from graphical to browser to apps to human language.

So far, the ability to make machines perform magic was restricted to a miniscule percentage of the population: the much-celebrated software engineers and programmers. The elite amongst them – mostly young, white and male, largely living in the West Coast of the US – built the world

---

[6] "Perplexity AI." 2025. https://www.perplexity.ai/.

around us, harnessing powerful computing machines to create new products and services that the rest of us used. With the sweeping democratization of computing that AI brings, potentially all eight billion of us become creators and builders, by instructing machines in our language to help us do our work for us. As this happens, we will need to reinforce and rebuild the human skills we have somehow lost along the way or sometimes ceded to machines. As Aneesh Raman and Mari Flynn write in the *New York Times*: "There have been just a handful of moments over the centuries when we have experienced a huge shift in the skills our economy values most. We are entering one such moment now. Technical and data skills that have been highly sought after for decades appear to be among the most exposed to advances in artificial intelligence. But other skills, particularly the people skills that we have long undervalued as soft, will very likely remain the most durable … work [will be] anchored more, not less, around human ability. A LinkedIn research estimates that 96 per cent of a software engineers' current skills, which is mainly how to write code in programming languages, will be taken over by AI. Seventy percent of executives said soft skills – interpersonal relationships, negotiating, motivating teams, etc. – were more important than highly technical AI skills."[7]

---

[7] Raman, Aneesh, and Maria Flynn. 2024. "Opinion | the A.I. Economy Will Make Jobs More Human." *The New York Times*, 14 February. https://tinyurl.com/yc6ub4jx.

Thus, it is the skills that made us originally human that will come to the fore. The use of language is one of the key ones – how we employ and manipulate the English language to write the best prompts, which tease out the most optimal answers, art or code from a machine. This will be followed by other key human skills, such as how we show the answers and data elicited from machines to others, how we persuade them to our point of view and leverage the relationships we have built with other people. The knowledge economy will give way to the relationship economy. As Minouche Shafik of Columbia University says: "In the past, jobs were about muscles. Now they're about brains, but in the future, they'll be about the heart."[8]

This will have profound implications for our educational system, which has been obsessively STEM-focused of late. We believe that the original subjects taught in our ancient monasteries and schools will come back: language and grammar, logic, mathematics, philosophy. Humanities, finally, will have a dominant say in technology, as it always should have been, as empathy, creativity and felicity with language becomes more valued. Raman and Flynn go on to write: "AI will probably give us fantastic tools that will help us outsource a lot of our current mental work. At the same time, A.I. will force us humans to double down on those talents and skills that only humans possess. The

---

[8] Ibid.

most important thing about A.I. may be that it shows us what it can't do and so reveals who we are and what we have to offer."[9]

Legendary software engineer Kent Beck, the author of *Extreme Programming*, posted a remarkable statement in 2023: "I have been reluctant to try ChatGPT," he said on X.[10] "Today I got over that reluctance. Now I understand why I was reluctant. The value of 90 per cent of my skills just dropped to $0. The leverage of the remaining 10 per cent went up 1000x. I need to recalibrate."

As AI becomes increasingly powerful, we all need to recalibrate. And we need to do so by becoming AI-literate.

Again, it is not AI that will replace you, but a human being using AI.

The above sentence, in many ways, is the raison d'être of this book. We urge you to be that AI-literate person, rather than the AI-ignorant. The choice is yours: you can either be the replacer or the replacee.

---

[9] Ibid.
[10] Beck, Kent. 2025. X (Formerly Twitter). 19 April. https://x.com/kentbeck/status/1648413998025707520.

This chapter was written with the help of Gemini, Claude Sonnet 4.7, ChatGPT 4o Canvas, and Perplexity.ai

4

The Future of AI and the Need for Literacy

"At some point, we may have to accept that machines are thinking at levels we can no longer comprehend."

— NICK BOSTROM

Some of you would know what BYOD means. Bring Your Own Device refers to a policy that allows employees to bring their own laptops and phones to work, a trend that is a delight to employees, but rankles IT and Security managers who have no choice but to work with disparate operating systems and brands while having to ensure they are safe and secure. It was primarily Apple which ignited this phenomenon as knowledge workers rebelled against the dull uniformity of Windows devices and wanted to bring their cool Apple MacBooks to work. This culture became more widespread in the iPhone and smartphone era, as a proliferation of various models led to fast adoption, the phones' personal nature compelling workers to bring their own phones to work, rather than use the ones issued by corporate IT departments. BYOD was an obvious take on BYOB – where the last "B" stands for booze – which restaurants and events used to encourage people to bring their own favourites.

The 2024 Microsoft and LinkedIn Work Trend Index Report coined the latest acronym in this lexicon – BYOAI, or Bring Your Own AI.[1] The report which polled 31,000 workers worldwide (check) had a startling revelation: 78 per cent, or almost four out of five, employees were bringing in their own AI tools to work, many times sneaking them in as apps on their smartphones or laptops, even when corporate policy did not allow them to! 46 per cent of employees had started using them six months back, and more than half were reluctant to admit to using AI tools because "AI makes them look replaceable." That's not all; the same report stated that two out of three leaders would not hire someone without "AI skills" and 77 per cent of hiring managers prefer a less experienced candidate with AI skills over a more experienced candidate without them! Correspondingly, 71 per cent of professionals believe AI will lead to early-career talents taking on greater responsibilities. Note that this report is a year old at the time of writing, a lifetime in this age of AI. The numbers would be even greater and more startling now. Regardless, it is clear that AI aptitude or literacy is a central hiring factor, with AI-literate professionals having a clear advantage in

---

[1] Microsoft. 2024. "AI at Work Is Here. Now Comes the Hard Part." www.microsoft.com. 8 May. https://tinyurl.com/2pu8anmc.

The Future of AI and the Need for Literacy

the job market and AI literacy a defining factor in career growth. Think of an accountant in the eighties still insisting on using tables, pen and paper to balance their books even as spreadsheets like Microsoft Excel took over the business world, specifically in the world of finance and accounting. The traditional accountant who refused to embrace this new technology would not last a week. In the same way, AI proficiency or literacy is no longer optional; it is as necessary as knowing how to work on a computer or using a spreadsheet or word processor. It is clear that the rapid adoption of AI in the workplace is not just changing how we work; it is reshaping hiring and talent management.

Organizations are beginning to prioritize AI skills over traditional experience, recognizing that AI-literate professionals bring a competitive advantage. We are on the cusp of a new era – one defined by AI and its rapidly evolving capabilities. AI is no longer a distant, futuristic technology, but an integral part of our daily lives. From chatbots that assist with customer service to AI-powered marketing campaigns and automated legal research, AI has seamlessly woven itself into the fabric of our work and personal lives. Most of us think of AI as ChatGPT, but there is a whole world much beyond it. In fact, ChatGPT, at last count in March 2025, had ten different models and sub-models in its dropdown options. There are new product and feature releases by OpenAI almost on a weekly basis. The stunning Image feature released on March 2025 produces realistic images, which seem to be designed by expert graphic designers. The images, especially those that looked like the ones designed by Studio Ghibli, attracted millions of users, leading to appeals by Sam Altman to slow down since the OpenAI "GPUS were melting"![2] Beyond ChatGPT are several foundation models from Google, Anthropic, X, Mistral, DeepSeek and many others. Then there are the hundreds and thousands of applications being built on top of these models. But the impact of AI and GenAI go beyond just helping us summarize documents, writing poems or designing recipes and ad copies. AI and GenAI both promise and threaten to impact jobs, work, society, geopolitics and even humanity.

As we wrote earlier, Gartner was prescient when it said that "AI is not just a trend or technology, but a fundamental shift in how humans and machines interact." The meta-trends of AI described below will hopefully lift you above the noise and speculation to help you understand why AI is the fundamental technology of our time and will impact the very foundational principles of humanity.

1. English is the New Coding

As Gen X was growing up, especially in countries like India, we were told that learning English was the passport to success. We did that faithfully, and were arguably successful in our careers and businesses. Our children, in

---

[2] Altman, Sam. X (*Formerly Twitter*), 2025, x.com/sama/status/1905296867145154688.

turn, are told that learning how to code is the passport to success, thus coding became the new English, leading to 10-year olds dragged to code camps to learn Python and JavaScript. With GenAI, this changes: every time we write an English prompt for ChatGPT or any of its ilk, we are actually "coding", i.e. giving it a set of instructions to perform some task for us, whether a summarization or a video creation or writing up an article. Except, now we're doing it in our natural human language, rather than the language of the machine. This is a very profound development, as it has the potential to democratize coding with, potentially, every educated person on earth being able to write code in their own natural language. Microsoft's Satya Nadella mused that instead of learning the machine's language, machines would have to learn ours; Jensen Huang of Nvidia was of the same opinion, saying that the true potential of AI is that none of us would have to learn how to code. Thus English, or any other natural language, becomes the new coding

2. AI is the New UI

AI becomes the new user interface (UI). Bill Gates presciently wrote in November 2023[3]: "… you won't have

---

[3] Gates, Bill. 2023. "AI Is about to Completely Change How You Use Computers." Gatesnotes.com. 9 November. https://www.gatesnotes.com/AI-agents.

to use different apps for different tasks. You'll simply tell your device, in everyday language, what you want to do." UI has defined how humans and machines have interacted with each other, evolving from the difficult UIs of machine language and DOS to GUI (Graphical User Interface), search bars, browsers and apps. Simpler and friendlier UI led to a faster, intuitive and more productive interaction with a machine. The AI-driven fundamental shift will lead to voice UI, as the spoken word becomes the new way to interact with machines, similar to interactions with other humans. We will chat with ChatGPT or Gemini to work with them on our day-to-day tasks. Our devices will morph with voice becoming the primary interface, rather than a large screen. The first proto devices are already out, even if not tremendously successful yet, like the Rabbit R1 and the AI Pin. But all in all, an AI assistant is fast becoming the new UI.

3. AI and Humans are the New Creators

GenAI is a cognitive technology, and can perform creative tasks like writing articles and poetry, as well as creating art. This has left many human creators deeply worried about their jobs and vocations, as creativity was supposed to be a uniquely human skill. We believe, however, that GenAI will boost human creativity. Take OpenAI's Sora, for instance:

When Sam Altman had teased it to us in 2024, he had invited creative prompts on X to instantly generate videos with the same. Indian entrepreneur Kunal Shah famously gave "A bicycle race on ocean with different animals as athletes riding the bicycles with drone camera view" and Sora produced a spectacularly creative video.[4] However, it was not Sora, which was being creative but Kunal, who would not have imagined a creation like this, unless he had a tool like Sora or Veo or Kling to manifest his innate human creativity. Thus, I believe, that the combination of humans and AI will give rise to a new era of creativity

4. AI Creates a New Customer

The Industrial Revolution brought with it the transactional industrial customer who rarely used technology, and the internet brought the digital comparison-driven social customer who searched and clicked her way through brands. A new kind of customer will emerge in this age of AI – someone who lives in the era of infinite hyper-personalized choice, has immersive and conversational interaction with brands, uses AI that anticipates her needs, helping her build a brand relationship that is collaborative rather than functional or emotional. This will mean a gut-

---

[4] Altman, Sam. 2025a. X (Formerly Twitter). https://tinyurl.com/cznszs48.

wrenching change in business and marketing, as industries race to adjust to this new reality.

Aspect	Industrial Customer	Digital Customer	AI Customer
Choice	Limited, standardized	Abundant, comparison-driven	Infinite, hyper-personalized
Interaction	Transactional, local	Omni-channel, social	Immersive, conversational
Technology Use	None or minimal	Reactive (search, click)	Proactive (anticipates needs)
Brand Relationship	Functional loyalty	Emotional and social loyalty	Collaborative partnership
Sustainability	Not a focus	Awareness growing	Integral to decisions

The New AI Customer

5. Agents are the New Platform

If 2023 was the year when ChatGPT reigned, and 2024 was when a thousand LLMs bloomed, 2025 will be the year of AI agents Bill Gates blogged about in 2023 with keen foresight: "In the next five years ... you'll simply tell your device, in everyday language, what you want to do ... and software will be able to respond personally because it will have a rich understanding of your life. This type of software – something that responds to natural language and can accomplish many different tasks based on its knowledge

The Future of AI and the Need for Literacy

of the user – is called an agent."[5] So, if you plan a vacation today, it means several hours spent tapping across multiple apps before you book a satisfactory itinerary. However, a future booking agent could select a hotel and airline based on your past preferences and pricing, design a daily itinerary based on your known interests and then proceed to book flights and restaurants, after you have given it the permission and the agency to do so. Sarah Hinkfuss of Bain Capital described this well: "We are used to 'pulling' information from computers, (AI agents will) 'push' finished work to us instead".[6] Hundreds of startups have heard his clarion call to build agents on top of the LLMs that Big Tech is rolling out – Microsoft with CoPilot Wave 2, Google with Gemini 2, SalesForce with AgentForce and so on. Minday scours the Internet and mines your preferences to find the best restaurant around you, while Relevance AI automates prospect meetings for harried sales reps. The CEO of the fintech firm Klarna announced that customer service agents built on OpenAI platforms have "replaced" 700 human agents. It is pertinent to note that

---

[5] Gates, Bill. 2023. "AI Is about to Completely Change How You Use Computers." Gatesnotes.com. 9 November. https://www.gatesnotes.com/AI-agents.

[6] Hinkfuss, Sarah. 2024. "To Succeed with AI, Give up Control." The Information. 30 May. https://tinyurl.com/3v8sa6a5. https://bit.ly/3Ye4reU

no employees were replaced here; but new contact centre roles were taken by AI agents, though under supervision by human beings.

6. SaaS is the New SaaS

Software-as-a-service will give way to service-as-a-software. AI will bundle up discrete steps in a typical enterprise workflow into an agentic AI software. Today, SaaS companies rent out software, which help humans in enterprises perform certain services. These "New SaaS" companies will sell the service instead, enabled by agentic AI. So, if QuickBooks sells a SaaS product today, which enables us to file our tax returns, agentic AI will focus on the end-service and file our tax returns instead, with minimal humans in the loop. This is a dramatic change, and Foundation Capital touts this as a $4.6 trillion opportunity, and a disruption to the structure of the industry and the jobs it provides.[7] Bill Gates warned us about this too in the same blog. "Agents are not only going to change how everyone interacts with computers," he wrote, "they're also going to upend the software industry." There has been

---

[7] Chen, Joanne. 2024. "AI Leads a Service-As-Software Paradigm Shift - Foundation Capital." Foundation Capital. 18 April. https://tinyurl.com/2rv62afx.

a lot of hand-wringing about GenAI not having "real" enterprise use case; it is agentic AI that will bring GenAI to the enterprise.

7. AI Agents Are Our New Colleagues

Agents will make their way into the workforce too. Today, a team comprises a group of humans, and the team leader's job is to know their strengths and weaknesses and help maximize their potential accordingly. This will change to a mixed team of humans and AI agents, where the leader's job will be to assign some tasks to humans and others to AI agents. Diversity in an organization will not only be across race and gender, but also across humans and AI, as in the Klarna example provided earlier. Jensen Huang and others are already considering bringing "millions of AI agents" into their companies, besides thousands of humans.[8] Experts are touting the new "one-person unicorn", a billion-dollar startup with one founder, and a team entirely made of AI agents.[9]

---

[8] Goel, Shubhangi. 2024. "Jensen Huang Wants Nvidia to Have 100 Million AI Assistants." Business Insider. 14 October. https://tinyurl.com/muzhzhdw.

[9] Tiwari, Kaushik. 2025. "The Rise of the One-Person Unicorn: How AI Agents Are Redefining Entrepreneurship." Forbes. 11 March. https://tinyurl.com/ykbj48x4.

8. Chat is the New Search

For too long, we have been subjected to the tyranny of the "10 blue links of Google", many of which are often tailored for what the advertiser wants, rather than the answers you are looking for. GenAI-based chat search engines like Perplexity.ai and OpenAI's SearchGPT promise to change this by scouring the web and providing you with answers you want in a conversational format, along with relevant sources. This is a completely novel, uncluttered and intuitive search experience, and has drawn even behemoths like Google and Microsoft to experiment with this new way to search. The trend is bigger than just moving away from a search bar to a chatbot. As the Internet exploded into billions of pages and sites, search became a way to organize the Internet and access it. This is where Google benefited immensely, by becoming an almost exclusive portal into the World Wide Web, and monetizing the traffic that poured into it. But the tectonic plates that underlie the Internet seem to be shifting now, with chats and conversations of ChatGPT and Perplexity, among others, becoming the way the Internet will be accessed and organized around. This new way to organize the web and all the information it contains will come under the purview of AI, with its chatbots, agents and a much more human-like intuitive interface. There are, however, obstacles along the way as a probabilistic GenAI-based search engine will never be as accurate as a deterministic database of a traditional search engine, but the trend is irreversible nonetheless.

9. Is the AI+ Human the New Human?

This is the only prediction that comes with a question mark since it is less certain and further out. Historians like Yuval Noah Harari have written eloquently about how the next phase in human evolution could be characterized by a combination of human and AI capabilities, harking back to the cyborgs of yore, with both biological and artificial (typically electronic or mechanical) parts integrated together. Homo deus, which will follow home sapiens, may have godlike powers (deus in Latin means god), with the help of new-age technologies like AI, biotech and brain-computer interfaces. However impressive this sounds, it could be a dystopian future, given the threat of obsolescence and loss of individuality. Not that this has deterred Elon Musk and others from working on brain-machine interfaces like Neuralink!

10. Ethics is the New Imperative

With these rapid advances in AI leading to major foundational shifts, the ethics around the technology needs to become as or more important than the technology itself. The pitfalls of unbridled AI are well known – bias, loss of privacy, surveillance, deepfakes, copyright infringement and plagiarism, adverse impact on jobs and meaningful work, environmental degradation and the looming threat of a malevolent super-intelligence itself. While the threats are many, the good news is that we have started to have debates and conversations around the ethics of AI quite early in the game than we've done for many other scientific-technological developments. With nuclear science, it took the horrific Hiroshima–Nagasaki bombings for people to sit up; with AI, the conversations have already begun, guidelines and regulations are being framed, and AI safety institutes are being established all over the world. This does not eliminate the threats, but does provide hope that humans will continue to control the technology, rather than the other way around, which is what has happened with social media.

11. AI is the New Literacy

This is the very core of our book, and we have detailed it across the forthcoming chapters. However, to summarize, we believe that the definition of literacy will change from reading, writing and arithmetic to also using GenAI tools like ChatGPT, Perplexity and others in order to become better at work and life. Companies are seeing a new trend, BYOAI or Bring Your Own AI, where 75 per cent of employees are carrying along their own AI to work, because

The Future of AI and the Need for Literacy

it helps them perform better.[10] Two-thirds of managers will not hire someone if they do not have the aptitude and curiosity to work with GenAI tools. Thus, managements across organizations, irrespective of sector or geography, need to frame the right policies and build enablers for all their employees to become AI-literate.

You can also scan the code to watch a video where one of the authors talks about all twelve AI trends for 2025 and beyond:

As you can tell, AI is a shape-shifting technology, which could have a profound impact on humanity. It is poised to change the relationship between humans and machines as English becomes the new coding language, and as it creates new kinds of customers and creators among us. 2025 will be the year of "Agentic AI" as AI agents become the new platform, SaaS gets redefined to service-as-a-software, teams morph to include AI, and it becomes the new cloud in enterprises.

Finally, it could define the future of humanity, a new

---

[10] Microsoft. 2024. "AI at Work Is Here. Now Comes the Hard Part." Www.microsoft.com. 8 May. https://tinyurl.com/2pu8anmc.

way to organize the internet, and as the ethics of it becomes equally or more important than the tech itself, most of us humans will have no choice but to become AI-literate.

In the unstoppable age of AI, our mindset must shift. We must learn to see AI as not a threat, but an enabler. Just as computers became an essential workplace tool, AI will soon be a fundamental part of how we work, create and innovate. The question is not whether AI will be adopted but how quickly individuals and organizations can attain AI literacy to stay ahead. The future belongs to those who embrace AI literacy. Will you be among them?

This chapter was written with the help of Claude Sonnet 4.7, ChatGPT 4o, and Perplexity.ai.

5

Building Your AI Literacy

"To understand AI is to understand the future. It's no longer optional."

— FEI FEI LEE

We've stated this before, but it bears repeating: it's not AI that will take your job, but a human being who has embraced AI.

The difference between being the human who takes the job, the "replacer", and the human whose job is taken, the "replacee", is AI literacy. We believe that the definition of literacy will change from knowing how to read, write and do basic arithmetic to how to do these *and* use AI tools available to us naturally and innately.

Again, as we explained earlier, literacy is not the same as training or upskilling. When you learn a language, you understand the patterns, structures and the grammar. Initially, you must learn them, but then you have to start using them instinctively. As you become literate in it, you can then compose a paragraph, write a poem or an essay and start doing sums in your head. The same is true for AI literacy – you will take some time to "get" it, but once you do, you will instinctively turn to an AI tool to help you do most of your work, hobbies like painting and writing and even personal activities like helping you with your child's homework. It is up to you how much of an expert you then want to become, where you can then think and reason with AI and even ask it to perform some tasks for you.

Stages of AI Literacy

The chart above, a modified version of the Microsoft LinkedIn Work Index Report 2023,[1] describes our approach to AI literacy. The report had four kinds of users:

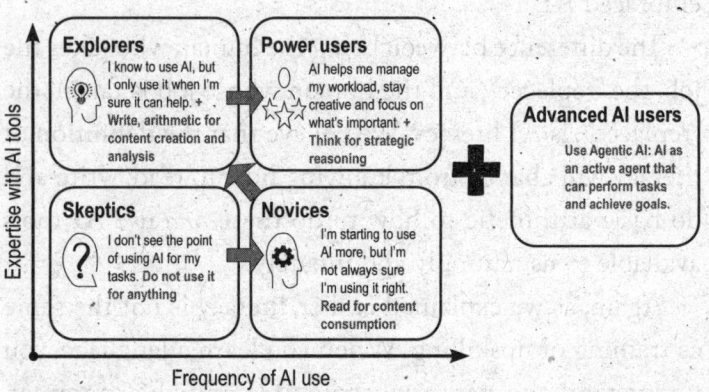

What Type of AI User Are You?

---

[1] Microsoft Work Trend Report 2023; https://www.microsoft.com/en-us/worklab/work-trend-index/will-ai-fix-work.

Sceptics, Novices, Explorers and Power Users. We have added a fifth one: Advanced AI Users. The chart categorizes users based on their proficiency, adoption and comfort levels with respect to AI, arranging these segments along a progression scale from low to high engagement.

The Sceptics are at the foundational level – these are individuals who hold significant reservations about using AI technologies. They question the practicality and relevance of AI in their daily tasks, showing minimal or no engagement with AI tools. Their scepticism often stems from concerns about reliability, privacy, perceived complexity or sometimes sheer inertia, making them resistant to adopting AI solutions.

Next are the Novices, who represent early-stage AI users. This group is beginning to experiment with AI, demonstrating openness but also uncertainty about optimal usage. They primarily use AI for passive or basic tasks such as content consumption or simple assistance in day-to-day activities like searching for a piece of information or news. Novices acknowledge AI's potential benefits but often lack confidence and comprehensive knowledge, resulting in sporadic and cautious use.

After this, we encounter the Explorers. This group has higher proficiency and more targeted engagement with AI tools. Explorers clearly understand when and how AI can be beneficial, applying the tools selectively and strategically. Their interactions typically include leveraging AI for email writing, basic arithmetic, content creation and analytical tasks. Though comfortable with AI, Explorers tend to remain cautious and only utilize these tools when assured of tangible benefits.

In the next category are the Power Users, who are characterized by frequent and confident AI usage, the tools integrated across various aspects of their workflows. Power Users rely extensively on AI to manage workloads, enhance productivity, foster creativity and prioritize significant tasks. Their interactions with AI are sophisticated, incorporating strategic reasoning and critical decision-making support. This group actively seeks ways to maximize AI's potential, demonstrating both comfort and proficiency.

At the highest level are Advanced AI Users, who clearly set themselves apart through their engagement with Agentic AI and how they use AI to think and do their daily tasks, some of which might be routine or repetitive. An example could be sending a calendar invite for a meeting, or writing a simple email reply or something more complex like an AI agent selecting a restaurant and ordering Thai food for dinner. These users perceive AI as more than just tools for task assistance; they actively employ AI systems capable of performing tasks independently, managing projects autonomously and proactively achieving specific objectives. Agentic AI represents a frontier where AI functions as a strategic partner, executing responsibilities and contributing directly to achieving defined goals.

This progression from sceptics to advanced AI users illustrates a clear trajectory in AI adoption – from resistance to cautious acceptance, selective utilization, strategic integration, and finally, autonomous task management – highlighting how users evolve in their interactions and proficiency with AI technologies.

The AI Literacy Roadmap (AILR)

The AILR is a simple roadmap which graduates you from a Novice to an advanced user, or whichever stage in between you would prefer. To make it easy and relatable, we have created the steps one would need to take to become literate in this age of AI.

Of course, you remember that literacy involves reading, writing and arithmetic. Advanced literacy requires thinking in the language, and getting it to do tasks and actions for you. Our simple model has the following five steps, based on the above, and described in the chart below:

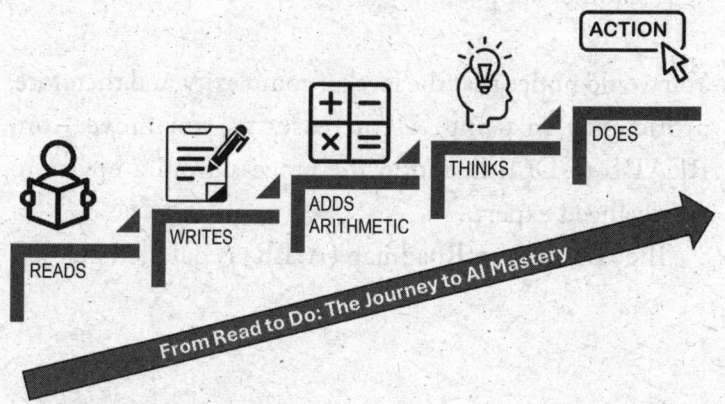

The AI Literacy Journey in Five Steps

Chart: The AI Literacy Roadmap
1. READS: using AI to better learn and absorb content, through translation, research, editing, summarization of long reports, etc.
2. WRITES: using AI to compose and write documents, marketing and branding messages, creating images, videos, presentations, emails, etc.
3. ADDS: using AI to automate core processes, analyse worksheets, decode markets and competition, data-driven decision-making, etc.
4. THINKS: using AI for thought leadership, new product development, innovation and brainstorming, knowledge management, strategic planning and using it as a second brain.
5. DOES: using AI to delegate to AI agents, orchestrate complex processes, execute and expedite work and customer support.

You would notice that the level of complexity, and therefore, proficiency in using AI increases as you move from READS to DOES, and in the process, from a novice to an advanced expert.

The AI Literacy Roadmap (AILR) is detailed below:

Step 1: READS

Real-Time Language Access
Edit and Enhance Content
Advanced AI Search and Research
Document Summarization
Sparring Partner

In the following chapter, we explore READS and each of the learnings described earlier. After introducing you to READS, through a live case study from our many bootcamps, we will show you how to use it for editing and enhancing a human-written sales pitch. You will learn about the tools you can use, the right prompts to write, best practices around this method, how to execute it safely and smart ways to review the output. In the same way, we will show you how to use AI to carry out document summarization, advanced research, etc.

Below is the capsule you need to master Step 1!

Real-time Language Translation
  Leverage AI to instantly translate languages, enabling seamless communication with global teams, partners, and clients, fostering a truly interconnected enterprices.
Edit and Enhance Content
  Transform existing content into multiple formats. Use AI to repurpose presentations, videos, and articles into engaging blogs, newsletters, and social media updates, maximizing reach and impact. Also, transcribe and analyze video content like meetings or conferences using AI and repurpose the content into various format.
Advanced AI Search and Research
  Conduct in-dept research and rapid fact-checking with AI-powered tools. Gain a competitive edge by accessing and synthesizing information faster than ever before.
Document Summarization
  Extract critical insights from extensive documents, reports, and meeting notes. AI-driven summarization accelerates comprehension and informs strategic decision-making.
Sparring Partner
  Description: Engage with AI as a thought partner to refine ideas, challenge assumptions, and explore alternative perspectives, fostering innovation and sharper strategic thinking.

Step 2: WRITES

Write Documents
Reach, Branding, Marketing
Images and Video Creation
Tailored Communication and Presentations
Email and Messaging
Speak and Collaborate

Like READS, WRITES too is self-explanatory: it helps you write and compose better using AI. In the WRITES chapter, we describe in detail how to use AI to write emails, texts and so on. Once again, we will specify the tools, prompts and best practices through a case study, so that you can learn, practise and attain proficiency.

Write Documents
  Draft, refine, and polish high-impact reports, proposals, and whitepapers and AI assistance. Achieve clarity, precision, and persuasive power in your written communication.
Reach, Branding and Marketing
  Craft compelling marketing content, including taglines, product descriptions, and social media posts, using AI. Enhance brand consistency and resonate with target audiences.
Images and Video Creation
  Design impactful visuals, including infographics, charts, and videos, with AI-powered tools. Enhance presentations, reports, and marketing materials with compelling storytelling. Also, produce high-quality videos for internal communication, marketing, or investor pitches, with AI-driven editing, subtitling, and effects.
Tailored Communication and Presentations
  Description: Develop visually engaging and persuasive presentations. Leverage AI to design slides, incorporate data visualizations, and create a compelling narrative flow.
Email and Messaging with AI
  Description: Craft concise, professional, and impactful emails and internal communications. Use AI to refine your language, tone, and overall message effectiveness.
Speak and Collaborate with AI
  Descrption: Use text-to-speech capabilities for various applications like audiobooks, voiceovers, or creating audio versions of your written concent.

Step 3: ADDS

Automate Core Processes
Decode Markets and Competition
Data-Driven Decision Making
Stakeholder Sentiment Analysis

Further details are in Chapter 8, and what ADDS will allow you to do is depicted in the chart below.

Automate Core Processes
  Automate repetitive tasks like report generation, meeting scheduling, and follow-ups. Reclaim valuable time for strategic initiatives and high-impact projects.
Decode Markets and Competition
  Employ AI to monitor competitor strategies, identify emerging market trends, and anticipate industry shifts. Gain a crucial advantage in strategic planning and positioning.
Data Driven Decision Making
  Analyze complex datasets, identify patterns, and generate actionable insights with AI. transform raw data into dynamic visualizations that inform strategic decisions.
Stakeholder Sentiment Analysis
  Utilize AI to gauge sentiment from employee feedback, customer reviews, and market chatter. Refine strategies, enhance communication, and build stronger relationships with stakeholders.

Step 4: THINKS

Thought Leadership
Human Resources and Human-Agent Optimization
Innovation and Brainstorming
New Product Development
Knowledge Management and Using AI as a Second Brain
Strategic Planning and Foresight

This is where it gets more interesting, as we now explore how to use AI as a second brain, one that functions tirelessly for us 24x7. Can we use AI to become a thought leader, to innovate new products or to make strategic five-year plans? Yes, the current tools allow us to do all these things, and we explain how in our THINKS chapter.

Time for your next capsule!

Thought Leadership
Leverage AI to identify emerging trends, analyze industry disruptions, and position your organization as a thought leader in its domain. Anticipate future challenges and opportunities.

Human Resources and Human-Agent Optimisation
Optimize talent acquisition, employee development, and performance management with AI. Enhance workforce productivity, engagement, and retention through data-driven insights.

Innovation and Brainstorming
Use AI to generate new ideas, explore diverse perspectives, and accelerate the innovatin process. Foster a culture of creativity and breakthrough thinking within your organization.

New Product Development
Leverage AI throughout the product development lifecycle, from ideation and design to testing and launch. Create innovative products that meet market needs and exceed customer.

Knowledge Management: Using AI as a Second Brain
Build a dynamic knowledge respository with AI. Capture, organize and retrieve critical information seamlessly, empowering your team with a collective "second brain" for enhanced decision-making.

Strategic Planning and Foresight
Embed AI-driven forecasting into long-term planning to pre-empt risks and seize opportunities.

Step 5: DOES

Delegate to AI Agents
Orchestrate Complex Processes
Execute and Expedite
Support and Customer Success

Finally, we reach the pinnacle of what AI can do. As we wrote in Chapter 10, 2025 is the year of Agentic AI, where

AI will not only tell us what to do, but do it for us. At the time of writing, there are some AI agents and proto-agents, which we describe in the DOES chapter. By the time the book reaches your hands, there will definitely be more advanced agents for you to employ.

But first, swallow another useful pill!

Delegate to AI Agents
    empower AI agents to handle routine tasks, manage schedules, and execute pre-defined workflows, freeing up human resources for more strategic endeavors.
Orchestrate Complex Processes
    Description: Utilize AI to monitor and manage complex operations, ensuring optimal performance, identifying potential issues, and proactively recommending solutions.
Execute and Expedite
    Accelerate project execution and enhance operational efficiency by deploying AI agents to automate tasks, streamline processes, and reduce turnaround times.
Support and Customer Success
    Deploy AI-powered chatbots and virtual assistants to provide instant support to customers, employees, and other stakeholders. Enhance service levels and build stronger relationships.

The ADAPT Framework: Five Principles to Keep in Mind

Even as you strive to learn AI and make it a habit, we propose five principles to aid your learning and usage journey; these will help you use AI effectively, consistently and safely. The framework provides a clear, structured approach to seamlessly integrating AI into daily activities and workflows. We have adapted this from Ethan Mollik's Four Principles[2]:

---

[2] Co-Intelligence: Living and Working with AI, 2 April 2024, Penguin Random House. Ethan Mollik. ISBN: 9780593716717.

Principle 1: **A**lways invite AI to the table
Principle 2: **D**ouble-check AI's output
Principle 3: **A**ct like AI is a colleague
Principle 4: **P**resent AI is the worst you'll see
Principle 5: **T**reasure your data like digital gold

Principle 1: Always Invite AI to the Table

The first principle emphasizes inclusivity in considering AI as part of any task or project. By consciously inviting AI into discussions and planning stages, users actively create opportunities for AI to demonstrate value. This habit encourages continuous exploration of AI's capabilities and fosters an innovative mindset where artificial intelligence becomes an integral part of decision-making processes.

Principle 2: Double-Check AI's Output

Ensuring accuracy and reliability is crucial in AI-driven outcomes. The second principle highlights the importance of critically evaluating AI-generated outputs. Users should consistently verify results, maintaining a balance between trust and scrutiny. By routinely validating AI's suggestions or outcomes, users enhance accuracy, mitigate potential errors and build deeper trust in AI tools over time.

Principle 3: Act Like AI is a Colleague

Viewing AI as a collaborative partner rather than merely a technological tool transforms the user–AI relationship. This third principle encourages you to adopt a cooperative and interactive approach, engaging AI as one would with human teammates. Treating AI as a colleague fosters a more nuanced understanding of its strengths and limitations, resulting in richer, more meaningful interactions that elevate overall productivity and creativity. The voice features in ChatGPT and other such AI tools make this principle even more effective and realistic.

Principle 4: Present AI is the Worst You'll See!

AI is moving super-fast, and every day there is a new AI tool better than the one you may have used yesterday. AI is only going to become more refined, and this makes the need to be AI-literate even more urgent! This is also true for our book: the tools described in the book were state-of-the-art when we wrote the manuscript. We are very sure that even more of them are available now.

Principle 5: Treasure Your Data Like Digital Gold

Data lies at the heart of effective AI integration, and thus, this final principle stresses the imperative of robust data protection and management. Valuing and safeguarding data as a critical asset ensures integrity and quality, directly influencing the effectiveness and reliability of AI tools. Responsible data stewardship not only preserves privacy and security but also significantly enhances AI's capability to deliver insightful, actionable results.

Implementing ADAPT for Maximum Impact

When applied consistently, the ADAPT framework enhances your AI literacy and promotes a culture of thoughtful, responsible AI use. It encourages individuals and organizations to remain proactive, adaptive and strategic, ensuring AI technologies serve as meaningful extensions of human capabilities rather than mere technological novelties.

By internalizing and practising these five principles, you will not only integrate AI seamlessly but also position yourself to fully leverage the transformative potential of artificial intelligence, driving sustained innovation and productivity in an increasingly AI-driven world.

This chapter was written with the help of Claude Sonnet 4.7, ChatGPT 4o Canvas and Gemini 2.0 Pro Experimental.

6

Foundational AI Literacy: READS

"Reading is still the main way that I both learn new things and test my understanding."

— BILL GATES

The Printing Press: A Revolutionary Shift

In the mid-fifteenth century, the world witnessed a revolutionary invention that would forever change the course of human history: the printing press. Before its advent, avenues for acquiring knowledge were limited, with information largely confined to the elite and difficult to disseminate widely. This lack of access restricted educational opportunities and stifled intellectual progress, as the vast majority of people had no means to obtain the information needed for personal or societal advancement. The spread of knowledge was slow and often confined to monastic scribes and scholars.

When Johannes Gutenberg invented the printing press around 1440, a revolutionary shift occurred, enabling the mass production of books and making written knowledge more widely available than ever before. This groundbreaking technology democratized knowledge and elevated human potential in three key ways:

1. **Widespread Access to Knowledge:** The printing press made books and information accessible to a broader audience, breaking down barriers and allowing more people to engage with written content.
2. **Acceleration of Learning:** The ability to produce and distribute books rapidly accelerated the spread of ideas and knowledge, leading to significant advancements in education and intellectual growth.
3. **Transformation of Society:** The widespread availability of books led to social and cultural shifts, as more people could engage with diverse perspectives and ideas.

Today, we stand at a similar inflection point in human history. Just as the printing press revolutionized access to knowledge over centuries, artificial intelligence is transforming how we process and understand information. But unlike the gradual impact of the printing press, AI's influence on reading, learning and comprehension is unfolding at an unprecedented pace, promising changes in years that previously took generations.

AI: A New Age of Information Accessibility

NVIDIA CEO Jensen Huang recently captured this shift, saying, *"If there's one thing I would encourage everybody to do, it's to go get yourself an AI tutor right away."*[1] He emphasized that AI has drastically reduced the barriers to understanding complex subjects, allowing individuals to carry a personal tutor with them at all times.

And this isn't just visionary talk. Research is already revealing the profound impact of AI-driven learning tools. The paper titled "LLMs as Academic Reading Companions: Extending HCI Through Synthetic Personae" details an exploratory study conducted by Celia Chen and Alex Leitch at the University of Maryland.[2] This study examined the impact of using the large language model Claude.ai as an academic reading companion. It compared students using Claude.ai to a control group and found tangible improvements, including higher retention of key concepts, more nuanced critical analysis and increased enthusiasm for engaging with complex texts among students who used the AI agent.

Another study titled "Implementing Learning Principles with a Personal AI Tutor: A Case Study", conducted at UniDistance Suisse, explored the integration of an AI tutor

---

[1] Burleigh, Emma. 2025. "Nvidia CEO Jensen Huang Says Everyone Should Get an AI Tutor Right Away." Fortune. 2 February. https://tinyurl.com/8ce3n9x2.

[2] Chen, Celia, and Alex Leitch. 2024. "LLMs as Academic Reading Companions: Extending HCI through Synthetic Personae." ArXiv.org. 2024. https://tinyurl.com/55352pkw.

into a neuroscience course.[3] The research demonstrated how AI-driven personalized tutoring can significantly enhance reading comprehension and knowledge retention, further highlighting AI's role in accelerating learning and information processing. The AI tutor utilized GPT-3 to generate microlearning questions and developed a dynamic neural-network model to personalize learning experiences for each student. The results indicated that students who actively engaged with the AI tutor achieved significantly higher grades, with an average improvement of up to 15 percentile points compared to a parallel course without the AI tutor.

The READS Framework: AI's Role in Reading and Learning

As AI continues to enhance the way we read and process information, it is emerging as more than just a tool and becoming an active participant in the learning experience. Through real-time assistance, personalized feedback and interactive engagement, AI is reshaping how individuals absorb and apply knowledge.

---

[3] Baillifard, Ambroise, Maxime Gabella, Pamela Banta Lavenex, and Corinna S Martarelli. 2023. "Implementing Learning Principles with a Personal AI Tutor: A Case Study." ArXiv.org. https://tinyurl.com/ypzk48t9.

Foundational AI Literacy: READS

To better capture this shift, we introduce the READS framework, which highlights five key ways in which AI is transforming reading, comprehension and knowledge retention. The READS framework breaks this transformation down into five core areas.

- **Real-Time Language Translation**: Breaking down language barriers and enabling seamless access to information across different languages.

- **Editing and Enhancing Content**: Improving clarity, grammar and style in writing to ensure effective communication.

- **Advanced AI Search and Research**: Helping users efficiently find, analyse and synthesize information from vast data sources.

- **Document Summarization**: Condensing large texts into digestible summaries, aiding comprehension and knowledge retention.

- **Sparring Partner**: Providing interactive discussions, critical analysis and debate-style engagement to deepen understanding.

Now, let's explore each component of this framework and its impact on knowledge acquisition.

Real-Time Language Translation

We intentionally begin with language translation for two crucial reasons. First, when machines learned to translate with human-like fluency, they didn't just bridge languages – they rewrote the rules of global communication and information processing, demonstrating AI's ability to comprehend and interpret human meaning at an unprecedented scale.

Second, machine translation was the proving ground for one of AI's most transformative breakthroughs: the transformer architecture introduced in the seminal paper "Attention is All You Need"[4] which launched today's GenAI revolution.[5] The authors of this paper chose the machine translation challenge because of its complexity, knowing that success in machine translation would showcase the full potential of their attention-based approach. This breakthrough was crucial, laying the foundation for many of today's AI-driven language applications. Beyond translation, the transformer architecture has enabled advancements in language modelling, summarization,

---

[4] Vaswani, Ashish, Noam Shazeer, Niki Parmar, Jakob Uszkoreit, Llion Jones, Aidan N Gomez, Lukasz Kaiser, and Illia Polosukhin. 2017. "Attention Is All You Need." ArXiv. June 12, 2017. https://arxiv.org/abs/1706.03762.

[5] Vaswani, Ashish, Noam Shazeer, Niki Parmar, Jakob Uszkoreit, Llion Jones, Aidan N. Gomez, Łukasz Kaiser, and Illia Polosukhin. 2017. "Attention Is All You Need." *Advances in Neural Information Processing Systems* 30 (4): 5998–6008.

question answering, sentiment analysis, text classification and content generation, transforming the way we interact with and process information.

The implications of this innovation for today's leaders and organizations are profound, as is evidenced in the following example from co-author Anuj Magazine's own life.

A Personal Case Study: Lost in Translation

It's funny how certain work moments stick with you. Back in 2009, I had just joined an end-user computing company, settling into my new role in Bangalore. About a week in, I received what seemed like a routine email from my boss in Tokyo. At first glance, nothing seemed out of the ordinary – the latest message was in English, discussing some product customization requirements for our Asian market rollout.

Then I scrolled down. What I found was a dense email chain stretching back nearly four months – and almost entirely in Japanese. I remember sitting at my desk that morning, coffee in hand, thinking, "Well, this is going to be interesting." Here was potentially important context about decisions and discussions I needed to understand, but to me, it was like an encrypted secret code. In 2009, this meant either waiting for translations or missing out on valuable background information.

Looking back in 2025, it's remarkable how much has changed in handling these cross-language communication challenges. Now, AI tools offer solutions that would have been unimaginable back then. For example, consider the following recommendation for those dealing with Japanese translation:

> ### AI Tool Recommendation
>
> For translating Japanese text, in our experiments, we found **ChatGPT** particularly useful because:
>
> - **Context Mastery:** ChatGPT excels at understanding Japanese cultural nuances and implicit meanings, producing more natural translations.
>
> - **Customizable Output:** Users can tailor translations for specific tones or industries, ensuring the message fits the intended context.
>
> - **Adaptive Capabilities:** The model's regular updates allow it to stay current with evolving language use and idiomatic expressions.

Suggested Prompt:
You are an expert business translator specializing in Japanese corporate communication. Help me translate this email chain with the following context:

Business Context:
- Department Type: [e.g. Product Development/ Operations]

Foundational AI Literacy: READS

- Communication Type: [e.g. Project update/Technical guidance]
- Organizational Structure:
  - Message Flow: [e.g. HQ to Regional/Team to Team]
  - Hierarchy Levels: [e.g. Management to Project Team]
- Timeframe: [Quarter/Year]

Translation Requirements:
- Business Accuracy
  - Maintain Japanese business etiquette levels
  - Preserve technical terms in both languages [Term-JP (Term-EN)]
  - Keep product references in generic form
  - Highlight any decision points
- Cultural Context
  - Note any implied deadlines or expectations
  - Flag cultural business customs
  - Mark subtle disagreements or concerns
- Action Items
  - Clearly mark action items
  - Note response expectations
  - Highlight dependencies

Output Format:
- [Reference ID]
- Message Level: [Thread Position Number]
- Communication Direction: [Up/Down/Lateral]

- Formality Level: [Casual/Standard/Formal/Ultra-formal]
- [Translated content]

Key Points:
- Decisions: [List]
- Action Items: [List]
- Follow-ups Required: [List]
- Cultural Context Notes: [List]
- Dependencies Identified: [List]

Additional Notes:
- Technical Terms Referenced: [List with both language versions]
- Implied Expectations: [List]
- Urgency Level: [Standard/Priority/Critical]
- Email Chain [copy email chain to be translated under thus section]

Best Practices Followed in the Prompt

This prompt is structured to ensure clarity, relevance and high-quality outputs by leveraging several prompting best practices:

- **Role Assignment:** Clearly defining the AI's role as an "expert business translator specializing in Japanese corporate communication" ensures that responses are tailored with the right expertise.
- **Context Specification:** The BUSINESS CONTEXT section ensures the AI understands the nature of

the communication, the hierarchy involved and the expected message flow, improving translation accuracy.
- **Clear Instructions & Requirements:** The TRANSLATION REQUIREMENTS section outlines **accuracy, cultural context and action items**, preventing misinterpretations and ensuring alignment with Japanese business etiquette.
- **Structured Output Format:** Providing a **detailed output format** ensures consistency, making it easier to extract key information like **decisions, action items and cultural nuances** without ambiguity.
- **Explicit Handling of Nuances:** The prompt **flags business customs, implied expectations and subtle disagreements**, which are often lost in direct translations.
- **Prioritization & Urgency Indicators:** By including an **Urgency Level,** the AI can highlight critical messages, ensuring the reader focuses on high-priority items first.

How to Keep Your Data Safe

- Safeguard your email data by **removing personal identifiers** before translation. Redact all employee names, contact details and proprietary information like product codes or internal project references.
- Only **share the minimal information** required for accurate translation – often you can extract just the

relevant passages rather than entire email chains.
- Before translation, check ChatGPT's settings menu to **disable model training with your data** to prevent your business communications from being used for AI model improvement.
- **Delete your conversation history** after completing the translation to eliminate any saved copies of sensitive information.

Smart Ways to Review AI Output

- **Cross-verify** critical elements of the translation **with a native Japanese speaker** (if possible), especially for cultural context interpretations, technical specifications, financial commitments and timeline-related content.
- **Look for inconsistencies** between what you know about the business context and what the translation suggests to catch potential misunderstandings.
- Document any corrections or validations made to the AI translation, noting specific changes for future reference.

Outcome

While in 2009, I had to navigate cross-language communication challenges without today's AI tools, modern professionals facing similar situations now have powerful solutions. By using the structured prompt approach outlined earlier with tools like ChatGPT, you can quickly process multilingual content while preserving cultural nuances and business context. What once took days and significant expense now takes minutes, allowing global teams to collaborate effectively regardless of language barriers. By following the data safety guidelines and review practices suggested, you can leverage these AI translation capabilities while maintaining appropriate security and accuracy standards.

Editing and Enhancing Content

Think about the last time you had to write something important at work – maybe it was announcing a major change to your team or presenting a new strategy to the board. The pressure's on. Every word matters. And there you are, staring at a blank screen, knowing that what you write could make or break trust, influence decisions and potentially shape your organization's future.

In the past, you'd probably spend hours crafting the perfect message, sending it through countless revision cycles and relying on a small army of people to polish every sentence. It was thorough, but painfully slow and resource-intensive. And let's be honest – sometimes all that editing would strip away your authentic voice, leaving you with something that felt more like corporate speak than your actual message.

Now, AI is completely reshaping how leaders communicate. It's not just about catching typos anymore – now, you have at your disposal a powerful tool that helps you enhance your message while keeping your unique voice intact. But what does this transformation actually look like in practice? How are professionals navigating this shift from traditional communication methods to AI-enhanced workflows? Let's look at the following example:

Elevating Executive Written Communication

In December 2024, during one of our AI bootcamps, we collaborated with a premier Indian hospitality chain – a brand renowned for its seamless guest experience and highly efficient operations. However, behind the polished facade, we uncovered a surprising challenge in executive communications, one that was quietly eroding leadership productivity.

The company's CEO had recently introduced a pre-meeting memo system, requiring senior executives to submit structured insights before leadership discussions. The intent was clear: improve decision-making, ensure better-prepared meetings and create a repository of institutional knowledge. But what seemed like a simple, structured process had unintended consequences.

During our session, we noticed that key decision-makers – the leaders – were preoccupied with drafting these memos. Several senior executives were distracted, splitting their attention between the AI bootcamp and their memo-writing duties. While they had strong operational insights, many found it challenging to structure their thoughts into polished documents, relying on extensive staff support for drafting and editing.

What was meant to be a tool for clarity and efficiency had become a burden. Executives with deep operational expertise were now spending a disproportionate amount of time refining language, structuring documents and aligning tone – tasks that didn't leverage their core strengths. The added workload created bottlenecks, slowing down decision-making instead of accelerating it. The irony? A process designed to enhance leadership meetings was now draining executive focus and productivity.

This scenario isn't unique to this organization. It's a common challenge that underlines a crucial question: How can we preserve the benefits of structured communication without sacrificing leadership bandwidth? The answer lies in leveraging AI tools strategically – not to replace human thought, but to amplify it and remove friction from the writing process.

> ### AI Tool Recommendation
>
> A tool like **ChatGPT Canvas** is a perfect fit here. It allows executives to quickly structure their thoughts using traditional means like pen, paper or MS Word documents, helping them retain control over their content. Then, instead of spending hours refining language and format, executives can use ChatGPT Canvas to brainstorm further ideas, get structured drafts with polished language (which the tool handles automatically) and make quick edits before submitting their memos.

How to Use ChatGPT Canvas

To enhance your executive memo using ChatGPT's Canvas feature, follow these streamlined steps:

1. **Input Memo and Activate Canvas:**
   - Paste your existing memo into ChatGPT.
   - Type "use canvas" to open the Canvas interface.
2. **Refine Content with AI Assistance:**
   - Highlight specific sections of your memo.
   - Request targeted edits, such as rephrasing or expanding on key points.
3. **Enhance Strategic Language:**
   - Use the "Adjust the length" tool (option accessible

via tools section at bottom-right) to condense or elaborate on sections, ensuring concise and impactful messaging.
4. **Incorporate Relevant References:**
   - Highlight areas where external data or references would strengthen your memo.
   - Instruct ChatGPT to suggest pertinent studies, statistics or industry insights to support your arguments.
5. **Finalize and Review:**
   - Apply the "Add final polish" feature to correct grammar, enhance clarity and ensure consistency throughout the memo.
   - Review the AI's suggestions, make necessary adjustments and confirm that the memo aligns with your strategic objectives.

Here's how ChatGPT Canvas enhances executive writing:
- **Reduces dependency on staff support** for drafting.
- **Ensures consistency in executive memos,** making leadership meetings more structured.
- **Frees up executive time** for decision-making rather than document formatting.

How to Keep Your Data Safe

- Access ChatGPT's data controls under settings **and**

- disable the "**Improve the model for everyone**" to prevent sensitive memo content from being used for AI training.
- Before processing executive memos, **redact specific financial figures, project code names and sensitive competitive strategy details** – you can use placeholders that maintain the memo's meaning without exposing actual data.
- After finalizing the memo, **clear your ChatGPT conversation history** to remove all traces of the document from the AI system.

Smart Ways to Review AI Output

- Compare the AI-enhanced memo against your original draft to **verify that no strategic intent or key insights were lost** in the refinement process.
- **Check that industry-specific terminology and company-specific context remains accurate** – AI may sometimes standardize language in ways that lose important nuance.
- **Review any sections where confidential strategy is discussed** to ensure the AI hasn't inadvertently introduced generic business language that dilutes your specific approach.
- Confirm that the **memo's tone aligns with your executive communication style** and company voice rather than sounding too standardized.

- Keep a record of which sections were AI-refined versus originally written to **maintain accountability for the document's content.**

Outcome
By integrating ChatGPT Canvas into their workflow, the leadership team significantly reduced the time spent on drafting and refining memos while maintaining the clarity and structure needed for high-impact decision-making. Executives were able to focus on the substance of their insights rather than getting caught up in formatting or language refinement. What was once a time-consuming bottleneck transformed into an efficient process, allowing senior leaders to channel their expertise where it mattered most – driving the business forward.

Advanced AI Search and Research

In boardrooms across the globe, the quality of decision-making often hinges on the depth and accuracy of available intelligence. But here's the reality: leaders are struggling to make sense of an overwhelming flood of information. Market reports pile up unread, competitive intelligence gets buried in endless emails, and valuable internal data sits untapped in various systems.

Think about it – you've got research teams working around the clock, using expensive business intelligence tools and more data than ever before. Yet, when someone asks a critical question in a meeting, you're still left scrambling to piece together insights from a dozen different sources. Time ticks by as your team digs through reports, combines spreadsheets and tries to connect the dots between conflicting pieces of information.

That's where advanced AI search is changing the game. It doesn't just find information for you – it distills the information down to clear, contextual insights that can actually drive decisions. Imagine instantly connecting the dots between market trends, competitor moves and your internal data to spot opportunities and risks before they become obvious to everyone else.

But what does this transformation look like in practice? Let's look at the following example.

Scaling Strategic Account Intelligence

In the winter of 2024, we partnered with one of the world's most esteemed account-based marketing (ABM) organizations, renowned for their meticulous five-step framework that consistently delivered exceptional results for B2B technology clients. As pioneers in their field, they were eager to harness AI's potential to transform their operations. This forward-thinking approach came at a crucial time.

Their account planners would spend weeks developing comprehensive profiles of each target account, meticulously analysing annual reports, press releases, LinkedIn updates, industry analyses and interview transcripts. In one case, a senior strategist spent three weeks diving deep into a single Fortune 100 company, working to connect the dots between the firm's public sustainability commitments, its internal technology initiatives and insights gathered from stakeholder interviews.

While this thorough approach consistently produced high-quality insights, the time investment was becoming a critical bottleneck. The agency recognized a clear challenge: how could they maintain their renowned strategic depth while meeting growing client demands? They needed to streamline their research process without compromising the quality that had built their reputation.

AI Tool Recommendation

For organizations facing complex research challenges, **Perplexity AI** stands out as a powerful solution due to the following reasons:

- **Efficiency and Speed**: Perplexity AI significantly reduces the time spent on research by providing quick access to relevant data and insights.
- **Comprehensive Insights**: The tool's ability to analyse up-to-date data from multiple sources, including annual reports, press releases, LinkedIn updates and industry analyses ensures that account profiles

are comprehensive and up-to-date. This helps in connecting the dots between different pieces of information, such as a company's sustainability commitments and technology initiatives.
- **Personalization and Contextual Understanding**: Perplexity AI's natural language processing capabilities enable it to understand complex queries and provide contextual insights. This is crucial for developing personalized account strategies that resonate with each client's unique needs and challenges.

How to Use Perplexity AI

1. **Initiate the Research Query:**
   - Input a comprehensive natural language query into Perplexity AI (https://www.perplexity.ai/), such as the suggested prompt below.
2. **Refine the Query:**
   - Utilize Perplexity AI's conversational capabilities to ask follow-up questions or request more detailed information on specific aspects of the company's strategies.
3. **Verify and Synthesize Information:**
   - Cross-reference the AI-generated insights with original sources provided by Perplexity AI to ensure accuracy and reliability.

4. **Develop Strategic Insights:**
   - Analyse the curated information to draw meaningful connections and develop actionable insights tailored to the target account.

Suggested Prompt

Act as a world-class researcher. Conduct a detailed analysis of [Company Name]'s public sustainability commitments and their internal technology initiatives. Your research should explore multiple dimensions, including:

1. **Corporate Sustainability Strategy:**
   - What sustainability goals has [Company Name] publicly committed to?
   - Are there specific targets related to carbon neutrality, energy efficiency, waste reduction or ethical sourcing?
   - How does the company report its sustainability progress (e.g. annual reports, sustainability reports, SEC filings or press releases)?
2. **Technology-Driven Sustainability Initiatives:**
   - What internal technology projects or investments has the company made to support these sustainability commitments?
   - Are they leveraging AI, IoT, blockchain or cloud computing for sustainability initiatives?
   - Have they implemented automation, predictive analytics or green data centres to optimize energy consumption?

3. **Key Stakeholder Perspectives and Industry Context:**
   - What have executives (CEO, CTO, CIO, Head of Sustainability) publicly stated about these commitments?
   - How do investors, industry analysts and regulatory bodies assess the company's sustainability efforts?
   - Are there any partnerships, alliances or joint ventures supporting their sustainability and technology goals?
4. **Competitive Benchmarking:**
   - How does [Company Name] compare to its competitors in terms of sustainability and technology adoption?
   - Are there similar or better approaches being adopted by industry leaders?
5. **Market Sentiment and Challenges:**
   - What are employees, customers and industry experts saying about the company's sustainability initiatives?
   - Have there been controversies, setbacks or challenges in implementing these initiatives?
   - Are there external pressures (e.g. regulatory requirements, activist investors, changing consumer expectations) influencing their strategy?
6. **Future Roadmap and Strategic Implications:**
   - What future technology investments has the company hinted at or publicly announced?
   - How do these initiatives align with broader industry trends and government sustainability policies?

Foundational AI Literacy: READS

- Are there upcoming regulatory or financial risks the company might face in executing its sustainability strategy?

Best Practices Followed in the Prompt

To understand what makes this prompt powerful, let's break down its three core strengths:

- **Clear Role Definition and Scope Setting:** The prompt begins by establishing a specific role ("world-class researcher") and defining a clear objective (analysing sustainability and tech initiatives). This guides the AI to adopt the right perspective and expertise level while maintaining focus on the specific task.
- **Structured Framework with Specific Questions:** Rather than asking broad, open-ended questions, the prompt breaks down the research into six distinct dimensions, each with targeted sub-questions. This hierarchical structure helps ensure comprehensive coverage while preventing the AI from drifting off-topic or missing crucial aspects.
- **Multi-dimensional Analysis Commands:** The prompt goes beyond surface-level research by explicitly requesting different types of analysis: factual data (sustainability goals), technical details (technology implementations), stakeholder perspectives, competitive context and future implications. This depth ensures the

AI provides a rich, nuanced analysis rather than just carrying out basic information-gathering.

How to Keep Your Data Safe

- When researching target accounts in Perplexity AI, **remove company-specific identifiers from your queries** – use descriptive terms instead of project codes.
- **Anonymize any data** you need to exclude by using generic terms like "Client A" instead of actual company names in your research queries.
- **Check Perplexity AI's privacy settings** and enable options that prevent your search data from being stored or used for training its algorithms.
- After completing your research, **clear your search history** and any saved queries containing client-specific information.

Smart Ways to Review AI Output

- **Verify all AI-generated competitor insights** against original sources by clicking through the citations Perplexity provides to ensure accurate interpretation.
- **Identify any sections where the AI has made assumptions** about company motives or strategy and highlight these for additional verification.
- **Compare the AI's analysis against your existing knowledge** of the target account to spot potential

inconsistencies or misinterpretations of company initiatives.
- **Look for vague statements** about sustainability commitments or technology initiatives and seek more specific language and evidence.

Outcome

By thoughtfully integrating Perplexity AI into their research process, the account-based marketing organization was able to maintain its commitment to strategic depth while significantly reducing the time investment required for account analysis. This approach ensures that they continue to deliver high-quality insights to their clients, even as they scale their operations to meet growing demand.

Document Summarization

Think about what's sitting in your inbox and on your desk right now – lengthy board reports, detailed market analyses, dense regulatory documents, countless strategic briefs. It's not just the volume that's overwhelming; it's also the weight of knowing that buried in those hundreds of pages might be the critical insight you need for your next big decision.

The reality is sobering: leaders today are spending nearly half their working hours just trying to stay on top of their reading load. Between endless email threads and crucial documents demanding attention, the better part of your week disappears into processing information rather than acting on it. That's not just a time management challenge; it's a strategic vulnerability. While you're heads-down sifting through documents, you're missing opportunities to think deeply about strategy, connect with your team or spot emerging market trends.

In such a situation, AI can not only help you to read faster and become more organized, but also enable you to quickly extract what matters from the mountain of information that demands your attention every day. This is why AI-powered document summarization is changing the game, helping leaders cut through the noise and focus on what truly matters.

Let's look at a couple of instances in which the organizations we worked with turned their challenge into an opportunity.

Helping CEO's Transform Technical Overload into Strategic Insight

In late 2024, during our AI bootcamp with one of India's leading energy and power backup solutions companies, we encountered a challenge emblematic of modern executive dilemmas. The CEO, a veteran with decades of industry experience, found herself at a crossroads. Despite her deep industry knowledge, she was drowning in an ocean of critical technical documents – detailed battery chemistry research papers, complex regulatory frameworks on grid integration and endless reports on emerging storage technologies.

Each document held potential game-changing insights for the company's future. A single missed detail in a technical paper could mean falling behind on a crucial technology trend. One overlooked regulation could impact their entire product roadmap. While these documents were filled with insights crucial for steering the company's future, their technical complexity and sheer volume made it nearly impossible for her to extract strategic implications quickly enough to stay ahead.

This predicament went far beyond the challenge of document review. In an industry where technology evolves at breakneck speed, delayed decisions could mean missed opportunities. The CEO needed to transform this flood of technical information into clear strategic direction – not just for sustainable growth, but for the company's survival in a market where today's technological decisions determine tomorrow's market leaders.

> ### AI Tool Recommendation
>
> **Claude Sonnet** emerges as the ideal solution for processing complex technical documentation. Unlike basic summarization tools, it can analyse entire PDF documents, including technical diagrams, data tables and embedded images, providing a complete understanding of technical content. What sets it apart is its ability to maintain context across multiple documents, extract key insights from complex technical jargon and present findings in clear, strategic terms.

How to Use Claude Sonnet

1. **Document Ingestion:**
   - Upload the relevant technical documents into Claude Sonnet's platform.
2. **Prompt Engineering:**
   - Craft specific prompts to guide the AI in generating concise summaries and highlighting key strategic insights.
3. **Review and Refinement:**
   - Evaluate the AI-generated outputs, refining prompts as necessary to ensure clarity and relevance.
4. **Integration into Decision-Making:**
   - Incorporate the distilled insights into strategic

planning sessions and executive decision-making processes.

Suggested Prompt

Act as a technical strategy advisor. Review these technical documents and provide a CEO-level summary focusing on:
- **Business Impact of Technology:**
  - What battery chemistry advancements could disrupt our current product line?
  - Which emerging storage technologies show commercial promise?
  - What's the implementation timeline and resource investment needed?
- **Regulatory Landscape:**
  - What new grid integration requirements affect our product roadmap?
  - Are there compliance deadlines we need to prepare for?
  - How do these regulations compare to our current standards?
- **Market Implications:**
  - Which developments give us competitive advantage?
  - What risks could impact our market position?
  - What strategic investments should we prioritize?

Best Prompting Practices Used

- **Role-Based Context:** Assigning the AI the role of a "technical strategy advisor" ensures insights are business-focused rather than purely technical.
- **Structured for Decision-Making:** Breaking down complex topics into specific questions that drive actionable insights.
- **Business–Technology Bridge:** Framing technical details in terms of strategic implications and market impact.

How to Keep Your Data Safe

- **Remove confidential information** like proprietary research data, unpublished innovations and market-sensitive projections before uploading technical documents.
- If possible, **share only necessary excerpts, not full reports**, to limit exposure.
- After receiving your summary, **delete the uploaded documents and conversation history** from Claude to eliminate retained copies.

Smart Ways to Review AI Output

- **Verify that Claude's interpretations of battery chemistry advancements match the original technical specifications** in your documents.

- **Compare** regulatory compliance requirements highlighted in the AI summary against the original regulatory text to confirm accurate representation.
- **Look for inconsistencies** between the AI's strategic recommendations and your current technical capabilities or market position.
- **Identify any vague statements** about implementation timelines or resource requirements and seek more specific information.

Outcome

By leveraging Claude Sonnet, the CEO could manage an overwhelming flood of technical documents into clear, actionable strategic insights. Instead of spending hours deciphering complex research papers and regulations, she could now access executive-level summaries that highlighted key opportunities, risks and market implications. What was once a challenge became a competitive advantage, allowing the leadership team to stay ahead of technological shifts, regulatory changes and emerging market trends with clarity and confidence.

Claude's Data Analysis Capabilities on PDF Files

- **Summarization:** Generating concise summaries of complex documents to convey essential information.
- **Viewing and Analysing Images:** Understanding and extracting insights from visual data such as diagrams, flowcharts and images in documents.
- **Viewing and Analysing Tables:** Interpreting and extracting insights from tabular data within the document.
- **Comparative Analysis:** Comparing different sections or types of information within the document to draw meaningful conclusions.
- **Trend Analysis:** Identifying patterns and trends in data over time or across different conditions presented in the document.
- **Extracting Key Metrics:** Focusing on specific quantitative insights from tables, charts or metrics provided.
- **Practical Applications and Recommendations:** Generating practical insights or recommendations based on the document's findings.

Foundational AI Literacy: READS

Making Sense of Breaking News Under Deadline

Also in late 2024, during our AI bootcamp for media professionals, a senior technology journalist from a prominent Indian media house shared a story that resonated with everyone in the room. Every quarter, when a US-based public technology company released its earnings, he faced a peculiar challenge due to the time zone difference. The earnings call would start at midnight IST, and he was expected to deliver a comprehensive story by the next morning's editorial meeting.

These weren't just numbers to report; each two-hour earnings call was a deep dive into the company's evolving story. Hidden in casual executive remarks could be hints of major strategy shifts. A slight change in investment focus could signal the next big industry trend. Missing these subtle cues wouldn't just result in an incomplete story; it could mean missing the bigger picture that his readers counted on him to see and interpret.

Once again, the pressure was intense. After staying up past 2 a.m. to catch every detail of the call, he would need to craft a thorough analysis of the company's performance, connecting financial metrics to broader market implications, all while fighting exhaustion. The next morning's deadline loomed over every minute spent transcribing and analysing. In a field where both speed and accuracy are non-negotiable, this physical and mental drain was becoming unsustainable.

But what if there was a way to understand the entire earnings call in a fraction of the time, without missing any crucial details?

> ### AI Tool Recommendation
>
> To address this challenge, integrating **NotebookLM's Audio Overviews** into the journalist's workflow would be highly beneficial. NotebookLM is an AI-powered research assistant developed by Google, designed to help users understand complex information by summarizing sources and providing relevant quotes. Its "Audio Overview" feature generates AI-driven discussions about the uploaded documents, summarizing key topics in a conversational format. This allows users to listen to concise summaries, making it easier to grasp essential information quickly.

How to Use Google's NotebookLM:

1. Login to https://notebooklm.google.com/.
2. Upload Earnings Call Transcripts:
   - After the earnings call, obtain the official transcript and upload it to NotebookLM.

3. **Generate Audio Overview:**
   - Use the "Audio Overview" feature to create a podcast-style summary of the transcript.
4. **Review Key Insights:**
   - Listen to the generated audio while on the commute to work.
   - Quickly grasp the main points, strategic announcements and financial highlights.

How to Keep Your Data Safe

When using Google NotebookLM, know the following about data privacy:
- NotebookLM does not use personal data for training. The system is designed to work with the sources you provide without using your personal information to train its AI models.
- Data processing is transparent. All analysis happens within your personal workspace, giving you control over how your documents are processed.
- Your uploaded transcripts and generated summaries should not be shared with third parties without your explicit consent.

Smart Ways to Review AI Output

- **Compare key financial metrics in the AI summary against the original transcript** to verify accurate reporting of earnings figures.

- **Analyse how the AI interpreted executive tone** and forward-looking statements against your own impression from the transcript.
- **Scan the original transcript's major** sections to ensure the AI summary didn't overlook significant segments or announcements.
- **Look for generic statements** about business strategy that need more specific clarification based on executives' actual comments.

Outcome

By incorporating NotebookLM's Audio Overviews into his workflow, the journalist drastically reduced the time spent processing earnings calls while ensuring no critical insights were missed. Instead of manually sifting through lengthy transcripts in the early hours of the morning, he could now listen to an AI-generated summary that highlighted key financial metrics, executive sentiment and strategic announcements. This allowed him to focus on analysis rather than transcription, improving both the depth and speed of his reporting. What was once an exhausting all-nighter transformed into an efficient, insight-driven process, ensuring he delivered high-quality journalism without compromising on accuracy or deadlines.

Sparring Partner

It's late at night, and you're staring at tomorrow's board presentation. The strategy looks solid on paper, but something doesn't feel quite right. You've run it by your team, but they're too close to the project. Your mentor would ask the right questions, but she's on vacation. The consulting firm that helped develop the strategy? They're already onto their next client.

These moments of needing a trusted thinking partner rarely come at convenient times. Whether it's pressure-testing a market entry strategy, rethinking organizational structure or evaluating a potential acquisition, leaders often find themselves needing someone to challenge their assumptions and offer fresh perspectives. But traditional advisors – board members, executive coaches, consultants – all come with their own constraints. They're either unavailable when you need them most, limited in their expertise or bring their own agendas to the table.

This is where AI steps in as a major game-changer. Imagine having a thinking partner who's always there, ready to engage with any business challenge you throw their way. No scheduling constraints. No political considerations. No preset frameworks or methodologies to sell. Just pure intellectual engagement focused on helping you make better decisions.

Let's look at a few instances where we saw firsthand the inspirational use of AI as a sparring partner in high-stakes situations.

Reimagining Student Comprehension by Learning to Teach

In 2024, during an AI bootcamp at one of India's premier management institutes, a distinguished professor of organizational behaviour shared a concern that might resonate with educators everywhere. Despite having bright, ambitious students who could ace exams and articulate theoretical frameworks perfectly, something wasn't clicking. The real test came during alumni conversations and corporate feedback. These same students, now in their early careers, were struggling to translate their academic knowledge into practical business decisions.

The disconnect was clear, but solving it wasn't simple. Traditional case discussions, while valuable, often felt rehearsed. Role-playing exercises could only go so far. Even industry internships, though crucial, were too high-stakes for the kind of experiential learning students needed. The professor had observed that students achieved their deepest understanding when they had to teach concepts to others, when they had to break down complex theories, anticipate questions and rebuild ideas from the ground up.

But herein lay the real challenge: Finding practice partners who could play the role of an engaged novice was nearly impossible. Peer-to-peer practice sessions quickly devolved into jargon-filled discussions since both parties were equally versed in management concepts. Teaching assistants were too familiar with the material to ask authentic beginner questions. And bringing in actual novices from outside the program wasn't scalable or sustainable. The result? Students were missing out on one of the most powerful ways to truly master their subject matter – teaching it to others.

What if students could have an always-available learning partner, one that could consistently play the role of an engaged beginner, ask probing questions and help them articulate complex concepts clearly? This is where AI opens up an intriguing possibility.

AI Tool Recommendation

To address this educational challenge, we recommend AI-As-A-Student, a CustomGPT created by AI&Beyond using ChatGPT's platform. This specialized GPT simulates a role-playing scenario where the user (student) practises teaching concepts to a novice learner (AI). By engaging with this simulated student, learners are compelled to simplify and clarify their explanations, ultimately deepening their own understanding.

How to Use AI&Beyond's AI-As-A-Student CustomGPT:

1. **Access the CustomGPT** via https://chatgpt.com/g/g-ZJBnoSSyw-ai-beyond-s-ai-as-a-student.
2. **Define Learning Objectives:**
   - Identify the key management concepts that students need to master and articulate clearly.
3. **Develop Practice Scenarios:**
   - Create realistic teaching scenarios where students can interact with the AI, explaining concepts and answering questions posed by the simulated novice.
4. **Monitor and Assess Interactions:**
   - Review the interactions between students and the AI to assess the clarity and accuracy of explanations, providing feedback for improvement.
5. **Iterate and Enhance:**
   - Continuously refine the AI's responses based on student performance and feedback to ensure ongoing relevance and challenge.

How to Keep Your Data Safe

- **Configure your CustomGPT** share setting as "Anyone with the link" to restrict usage to authorized students and faculty only.
- **Instruct students to use general business scenarios** rather than real company cases that might contain

confidential information.
- **Avoid uploading sensitive teaching materials** containing proprietary frameworks or unpublished research to the CustomGPT.
- **Establish a clear usage policy for students** that prohibits entering personally identifiable information during their AI teaching practice.

Smart Ways to Review AI Output

1. After each simulated teaching session, critically evaluate how well you explained complex concepts in simple terms. Identify areas where the AI "student" requested clarification, as these most likely indicate concepts that need further refinement in your explanations.
2. Pay attention to the types of questions the AI generates. These can reveal common misconceptions or areas of difficulty that real students might encounter, helping you prepare more comprehensive explanations for future teaching scenarios.
3. Regularly review your explanations for the same concept across multiple AI interactions. This helps you identify improvements in your teaching approach and ensures consistency in your ability to articulate key management theories clearly.

Outcome
By integrating AI-As-A-Student into the learning process, students gained an invaluable tool for reinforcing their understanding through teaching. Instead of passively absorbing information, they were actively engaged in explaining concepts, responding to probing questions and refining their clarity of thought. The AI provided a scalable, always-available learning partner that challenged them to articulate ideas in ways a true beginner would understand. As a result, students not only improved their theoretical grasp of management concepts but also developed the communication skills needed to apply them in real-world business scenarios, bridging the gap between academic knowledge and professional execution.

This chapter was written with the help of ChatGPT 4o Canvas and Perplexity.ai.

7

Intermediate AI Literacy: WRITES

"If I had more time, I would have written a shorter letter."
— BLAISE PASCAL

Knowledge on Leaves: The Legacy of Palm-Leaf Manuscripts

In ancient India, knowledge was preserved through a sophisticated tradition of palm-leaf (*patra* in Sanskrit) manuscript writing, where skilled practitioners – artisans, scholars, monks – meticulously inscribed texts onto dried palm leaves using specialized metal styluses. Creating these artistic masterpieces required immense patience, often taking months or years as artisans prepared leaves through elaborate processes like drying, boiling, smoothing and treating with oils such as lemon grass oil to prevent deterioration.[1] These manuscripts, inscribed in languages

---

[1] Sunder, Kalpana. 2023. "Kerala Museum Gives India's Historic Palm Leaf Manuscripts a New Home." The National. 17 February. https://tinyurl.com/32ypza32.

like Sanskrit, Tamil and Pali, contained diverse forms of knowledge spanning philosophy, science, literature and religion. Centres like Nalanda and Takshashila played a significant role in disseminating knowledge during this era and played a pivotal role in cultivating intellectual inquiry and debate.

As historian Romila Thapar notes in her work on ancient Indian intellectual traditions, writing supplemented oral transmission rather than replacing it entirely.[2] This dual approach transformed how knowledge was structured and shared while maintaining India's rich tradition of debate and inquiry. However, the laborious process of manuscript production posed significant challenges, limiting the accessibility and dissemination of written knowledge.

The Stenographer's Pool: Efficiency and the Democratization of Dictation

As centuries passed, the labour-intensive process of manual inscription gave way to new technologies that sought to address the growing demand for faster and more efficient methods of writing.

---

[2] Library of Congress and Sponsoring Body John W. Kluge Center. 2009. *Romila Thapar: Perceptions of the Past in Early India*. Washington, D.C.: Library of Congress, 5 December. Video. https://www.loc.gov/item/2021688241/.

Fast forward to the late nineteenth and early twentieth centuries. The invention of the typewriter, followed by the rise of stenography and dictation, marked a significant shift. While not as revolutionary as the printing press in terms of *distribution*, these technologies dramatically increased the *speed* and *efficiency* of writing itself. The stenographer's pool became a common sight in offices, transforming spoken words into typed documents with remarkable speed. This era saw the rise of business correspondence, mass-produced memos and a general acceleration in the volume of written communication. The act of writing, while still requiring skill, became more accessible. The focus shifted from the painstaking artistry of the individual letter to the rapid production of clear, concise text. This transition marked a pivotal moment in history when writing shifted from an elite art form to a practical tool for everyday communication, democratizing creation while still requiring specialized skills.

AI: The Dawn of Algorithmic Authorship

Just as stenography revolutionized how quickly ideas could be transcribed into text, artificial intelligence is now transforming the very nature of authorship itself. Building on humanity's long tradition of innovation in writing, AI represents the next frontier in our journey towards creating and sharing knowledge.

With the power of AI in content production, we are moving from:
- Recording thoughts to generating them in diverse forms
- Transcribing to composing
- Editing to augmenting content

AI tools don't simply correct grammar or suggest synonyms; they can draft entire documents, create compelling narratives, craft persuasive marketing copy, create and edit images and even generate creative content like poems and scripts.

This isn't mere speculation. A recent study titled "The Widespread Adoption of Large Language Model-Assisted Writing Across Society" by Liang et al analysed millions of documents across diverse sectors – including consumer complaints, corporate communications, job postings, as well as United Nations press releases.[3] Their findings reveal a dramatic surge in LLM-assisted writing following the release of ChatGPT, with significant adoption rates across all examined domains, highlighting the pervasive impact of AI on written communication. For instance, by September 2024, 18 per cent of financial consumer complaints, 24 per cent of press releases, 15 per cent of job postings and 14 per cent of UN press releases exhibited signs of LLM-generated writing.

---

[3] Liang, Weixin, Yaohui Zhang, Mihai Codreanu, Jiayu Wang, Hancheng Cao, and James Zou. 2025. "The Widespread Adoption of Large Language Model-Assisted Writing across Society." ArXiv.org. 17 February. https://tinyurl.com/mt3pxrkc.

This chapter will explore what it means to create in the age of AI by leveraging the WRITES framework.

WRITES: The Six Pillars of AI-Powered Content Creation

The WRITES framework outlines six core capabilities that define AI's role in the creation process. The acronym stands for:

- **Writing Documents:** This is the foundational element. Writing with AI goes beyond simple word processing; AI can structure arguments, tailor tone and adapt to specific writing styles.

- **Reach, Branding, Marketing:** This encompasses crafting compelling marketing materials, developing consistent brand voice guidelines and creating content specifically tailored to resonate with target audiences.

- **Image and Video Creation:** AI's creative capabilities aren't limited to just text. It can generate original images, edit existing visuals and even create videos from scratch or based on textual prompts.

- **Tailored Communication and Presentations:** AI can analyze audience data to create customized messages, presentations and reports that are specifically designed to resonate with individual recipients or groups.

- **Email and Messaging:** AI can streamline communication workflows by drafting emails, summarizing long threads and even managing responses.
- **Speaking and Collaboration:** AI facilitates voice-based interaction, enabling users to dictate text, control applications with voice commands and participate in real-time collaborative writing and editing sessions.

In essence, each part of the WRITES framework represents a democratization of content creation. The skills that once took years to master – crafting compelling narratives, designing visually appealing materials, adapting communication to different audiences – are now becoming accessible through AI-powered tools. This doesn't eliminate the need for human creativity and critical thinking; rather, it *amplifies* those skills, allowing writers to focus on the higher-level aspects of strategy, ideation and refinement.

Now, let's explore each component of this framework and its impact on content creation and authorship.

Writing Documents

In today's knowledge economy, the ability to craft compelling documents isn't just a skill – it's a strategic advantage. Yet, the reality for most professionals is sobering: hours spent staring at blank screens, struggling to transform complex ideas into clear prose, followed by endless revision cycles that drain productivity and creative energy.

Consider your last major report or proposal. How much time did you spend wrestling with structure, refining language or ensuring consistency across dozens of pages? For most leaders, document creation remains one of the most time-intensive yet under-examined aspects of their workflow — a necessary but often painful process of translating expertise into meaningful impact.

This is where AI is fundamentally changing the equation. We're witnessing a shift from documents as labor-intensive projects to dynamic collaborations between human expertise and machine assistance. The most AI-aware individuals aren't just using AI to speed up writing — they're reimagining the entire document creation process, from initial brainstorming to final polishing.

But what does this transformation look like in practice? How are professionals leveraging AI to create higher-quality writings in a fraction of the time? Let's explore a compelling example that illustrates the power of AI-assisted writing.

Crafting Authentic Executive Voices

One of our engagements was with a top Indian PR agency, renowned for their world-class public relations work. Among their many high-impact services, one of the most valued offerings was crafting communications for senior executives at Fortune 500 companies and fast-growing startups. Their approach was meticulous. Teams would immerse themselves in a CEO's past interviews, speeches and articles, spending countless hours to ensure each piece of communication perfectly reflected their client's unique style.

One project really showed us what this meant in practice. The team took several days and went through fifteen revisions just to nail down a tech founder's special way of breaking down complex ideas. While this deep attention to detail had attracted an impressive list of clients, it was also raising some red flags.

Their traditional approach – using multiple writers and editors to study and mirror executive communication styles – was becoming harder to sustain. Clients wanted faster turnarounds but weren't willing to compromise on quality or authenticity. The agency was facing a clear challenge: how could they keep delivering the genuine, high-quality executive communications they were known for while keeping up with the increasing pressure for speed?

Intermediate AI Literacy: WRITES

AI Tool Recommendation

To address this challenge, integrating an AI tool like **Claude**, developed by Anthropic, could be transformative. Claude's **Custom Styles** feature allows users to train the AI to emulate specific writing styles by providing sample content. This capability enables the AI to generate text that closely mirrors the unique voice and styles of different executives.

Additionally, Claude provides the unique ability to edit and refine these styles over time, allowing users to continuously improve personalization as their communication needs evolve – a flexibility rarely found in other AI writing assistants.

How to Use Claude Styles

1. **Access the Styles Feature:**
   - Log in to your Claude AI account via https://claude.ai/.
   - Navigate to the "Choose Style" section, typically found under the prompt box.
2. **Create a New Custom Style:**
   - Select the option to create a new style.

- Upload sample content that exemplifies the CEO's communication style, such as past speeches, interviews or articles.
3. **Define Style Parameters:**
    - Provide specific instructions detailing the desired tone, formality and any particular linguistic nuances. For example, note preferences for simplicity, use of analogies or a conversational tone.
4. **Test and Refine the Style:**
    - Generate a draft press release or communication using the newly created style.
    - Review the output to ensure it accurately reflects the intended voice.
    - Make necessary adjustments to the style parameters based on this review.
5. **Implement in Workflow:**
    - Once satisfied with the custom style, integrate it into your content creation process.

Here's how Claude's Style feature transforms executive communications:
- **Preserves brand consistency across leadership communications,** ensuring that even when multiple executives are communicating, the organization maintains a unified voice while honouring individual stylistic nuances.
- **Dramatically reduces the editorial burden on communications teams,** who no longer need to

spend hours revising drafts to match executive voices – allowing them to focus on strategic messaging rather than stylistic adjustments.
- **Facilitates rapid scaling of personalized communications** during high-volume periods like product launches or situations requiring crisis responses, when executives need to address multiple stakeholders with authentic-sounding messages quickly.

How to Keep Your Data Safe

- Claude does not store or use your conversations for model training by default, providing an additional layer of data security without requiring any special settings.
- Log out of Claude after each session, especially on shared agency devices.
- Ensure any personal identifiers within sample executive content are replaced with generic terms before uploading to Claude.
- After completing projects, regularly delete saved conversations and drafts from Claude to prevent unauthorized access to client materials.

Smart Ways to Review AI Output

- Editors should review AI-generated drafts to ensure they accurately reflect the intended message and adhere to the client's style.

- Identify any language that seems too formal or informal compared to the executive's usual communication style and adjust accordingly.
- Cross-check the content to confirm that it authentically represents the executive's voice and does not include any inaccuracies or misrepresentations.
- Ensure that the content aligns with ethical standards and does not inadvertently include biased or inappropriate language.
- Obtain final approval from the client before dissemination to ensure satisfaction and accuracy.

Outcome

By integrating Claude Styles into their workflow, the PR agency was able to maintain the authenticity of executive voices while dramatically improving turnaround time. Instead of spending days manually refining drafts, teams could now generate highly personalized content in minutes, preserving each executive's unique style while streamlining the revision process. This shift allowed them to meet growing client demands without sacrificing quality, freeing up time for higher-level strategic messaging. What was once an unsustainable editorial burden became a scalable, efficient process, ensuring the agency stayed ahead in a fast-paced industry where precision and speed are equally critical.

Intermediate AI Literacy: WRITES

Reach, Branding, Marketing

Every brand competes for attention in an increasingly crowded digital landscape. Whether you're launching a new product, rebranding an existing one or driving engagement through social media, the right message makes all the difference. But consumers today are overwhelmed with content – emails, ads, social media posts and videos flood their feeds every second. Attention spans are shorter, expectations are higher and brand loyalty is harder to earn. The challenge? Breaking through the noise with content that not only grabs attention but also resonates, builds trust and reinforces your brand identity.

For decades, marketing teams have relied on intuition, experience and A/B testing to craft compelling campaigns. But the sheer volume of platforms, shifting consumer behaviours and the speed of content consumption have made traditional methods less effective. What worked yesterday may be irrelevant today. Marketers must now deliver the right message to the right audience at the right time – without endless manual iteration.

AI is revolutionizing how brands connect with their audiences. From generating ad copy that converts to creating personalized content at scale, AI is making marketing not just faster, but also smarter. But what does this look like in action?

Let's explore an example.

Scaling Personalized Content for B2B Customer Journeys

At an industry forum round-table discussion, the Chief Marketing Officer (CMO) of a cybersecurity product-focused enterprise software company described a challenge that perfectly illustrated the modern B2B marketing dilemma.

"Our sales cycles last six–ten months, with buying committees of six–eight stakeholders across technical, financial and executive roles," she explained. "Each stakeholder needs different content at different stages – technical whitepapers for IT, ROI analyses for finance, strategic vision for executives. We know personalization drives conversion, but it's hard to find content experts who can create custom content for every role at every stage for every industry we serve."

Their marketing team was caught in a challenging situation. Generic content or some basic level of personalization failed to engage prospects, while fully customized content couldn't scale across their diverse customer base. They had high-quality templates and messaging frameworks but lacked the bandwidth to tailor them for thousands of specific customer contexts.

The CMO gave this issue the highest priority as the company's product portfolio was being expanded. Each new solution required fresh content across the entire customer journey. Their content team had got stuck at a bottleneck, with sales representatives waiting weeks for customized materials for important prospects.

The real pain point wasn't content quality – it was the ability to scale personalization without proportionally scaling their marketing team. The CMO needed a solution that could multiply their content team's capacity while maintaining the strategic and technical accuracy their B2B customers expected.

AI Tool Recommendation

In our experiments, we have found **ChatGPT 4.5** to be one of the best solutions for scaling personalized content in B2B customer journeys. ChatGPT 4.5 distinguishes itself with advanced pattern recognition and creative insight generation, enabling it to produce nuanced, contextually aware content tailored to diverse audiences. Its enhanced emotional intelligence facilitates more natural and intuitive interactions, making it adept at tasks requiring empathy and human-like understanding. Its compatibility with existing brand templates and frameworks allows marketing teams to rapidly customize materials without sacrificing quality or accuracy, addressing the bottleneck of manual content creation.

Suggested Prompt

I'm a marketing team member at a cybersecurity enterprise software company with limited bandwidth. We need to quickly generate high-quality, personalized content for diverse stakeholders across multiple industries throughout a 6–10 month sales cycle.

Solution Focus
- Product/Solution: [Specific cybersecurity product or solution, e.g. threat detection software]
- Core Value Proposition: [Briefly describe how this solution addresses cybersecurity challenges, e.g. "Enhanced threat detection and response capabilities"]
- Key Differentiators:
  - [Unique feature, e.g. AI-driven threat analysis]
  - [Competitive advantage, e.g. faster response times]
  - [Innovative technology, e.g. cloud-based security solutions]

Customization Parameters
- Target Industry: [Specific industry, e.g. finance, healthcare]
- Prospect Company Profile:
  - Size: [Small/Medium/Large]
  - Market Position: [Leader/Challenger/Niche]
  - Relevant Challenges: [Compliance risks, data breaches]

- Stakeholder Role: [Technical (IT), Financial (CFO), Executive (CEO)]
- Buying Journey Stage: [Awareness, consideration, decision]

Content Requirements

- Format: [Case study, whitepaper, executive summary, ROI analysis]
- Length: [Approximate word count or page length, e.g. 2–3 pages]
- Technical Depth: [Basic, intermediate, advanced]
- Required Elements:
  - [Specific components to include, e.g. industry benchmarks, customer testimonials]
- Call to Action: [Desired next step, e.g. schedule a demo, contact a sales representative]

Please create tailored content that:
- Addresses Specific Pain Points: For this industry and role, highlight how our solution mitigates common cybersecurity challenges.
- Adapts Technical Language: Ensure the content is accessible and relevant to the stakeholder's technical background.
- Provides Relevant Examples or Use Cases: Include scenarios or case studies that demonstrate the solution's effectiveness in similar contexts.

- Incorporates Industry-Specific Terminology and Frameworks: Use language and concepts familiar to the target audience.
- Aligns with the Buying Journey Stage: Tailor the content to resonate with the prospect's current stage of engagement.
- Includes Suggestions for Data Points or Proof Elements: Recommend metrics or evidence that would strengthen the content's persuasive impact.

Prompting Best Practices Used

- **Staged Complexity Signaling:** The prompt uses nested bullet hierarchies to create a mental model of complex relationships before content creation begins. This signals to the AI the exact level of detail expected for each component, creating a structured information architecture that guides the AI's reasoning process rather than simply listing requirements.
- **Pre-emptive Constraint Framing:** Instead of just stating what to include, the prompt identifies the actual business constraints ("limited bandwidth") upfront, priming the AI to optimize its response for efficiency and scalability. This context-setting before making requests creates a problem-solving mindset rather than just a content generation task.
- **Multi-dimensional Audience Triangulation:** The prompt doesn't just specify an audience but in fact

creates a four-axis audience model (industry + company profile + stakeholder role + journey stage) that forces the AI to consider intersecting perspectives simultaneously. This approach generates content that addresses complex B2B buying committees rather than simplistic buyer personas.

How to Keep Your Data Safe

- Navigate to the Settings menu in ChatGPT, then go to the Data Controls section. **Turn off the "Improve the model for everyone" toggle** to prevent OpenAI from using your prompts for model training. This ensures your conversations remain private and are not incorporated into future AI updates.
- **Activate Temporary Chat** mode before starting a session with sensitive data. This feature prevents the conversation from being saved in your chat history and ensures it is excluded from model training, offering a secure way to interact with ChatGPT without compromising privacy.
- **For long-term control over data usage, submit a formal request via OpenAI's privacy portal** asking them not to use your data for training purposes. You can do so via https://privacy.openai.com/. This option requires verification, but provides an added layer of assurance for sensitive or proprietary information.

Smart Ways to Review AI Output

- Check claims and product information against official internal documentation; involve sales engineers or product experts. **Verifying technical accuracy is crucial.**
- **Ensure messaging, tone and technical depth are consistent** and appropriate across different pieces generated for various stakeholders (e.g., CFO vs. IT Manager).
- **Confirm the content directly addresses the specific pain points,** industry context and buying stage of the target stakeholder.
- **Refine vague marketing statements into specific, quantifiable benefits** relevant to your cybersecurity offerings.
- Check that the desired next step is obvious and appropriate for the content format and audience. **Ensure clear calls to action.**

Outcome

By integrating ChatGPT 4.5 into their content strategy, the marketing team overcame the bottleneck of scaling personalized content without increasing headcount. With the ability to customize technical depth, industry language and business impact messaging, ChatGPT 4.5 transformed a slow, resource-intensive process into an agile, scalable system. This shift allowed sales teams to engage prospects more effectively, accelerating conversions while maintaining the depth and precision required for B2B decision-makers.

Image and Video Creation

Visual communication has always been powerful, but today it's become absolutely essential. In a world where attention spans are measured in seconds and information overload is constant, the ability to communicate through compelling visuals isn't just nice to have – it's necessary for survival.

Think about your organization's current approach to visual content. How many great ideas never made it past the planning stage because you lacked the design resources? How often have you settled for generic stock images that failed to capture your unique message? For most organizations, visual creation remains a bottleneck – a specialized skill set dependent on limited creative resources and technical expertise.

AI is now thoroughly clearing these hurdles. We're witnessing a fundamental democratization of visual creativity, where the gap between imagination and execution is shrinking dramatically. Leaders no longer need to choose between quality and speed, or between creative control and technical capability. Instead, they're using AI to bring their visual ideas to life with unprecedented ease and flexibility.

But what does this revolution in visual creation look like in practice? How are organizations leveraging AI to transform their visual storytelling capabilities? Let's examine another example.

The Professor's Visualization Dilemma

During our AI bootcamp at a top management institute in India, several professors shared a common frustration over tea. "I spent four hours last night just trying to make my supply chain management slides visually appealing," one of them remarked.

The group quickly agreed this was an unexpressed pain point. Whether teaching marketing analytics, financial modeling or leadership theory, these domain experts were spending 25–30 per cent of their preparation time not on developing content but on visualization.

"Our students expect engaging visuals," one professor noted, "but we're subject matter experts, not designers." This challenge was particularly evident with technical subjects, where complex frameworks and multi-layered concepts needed clear visual representation that maintained student attention.

The professors found themselves in a difficult position – should they sacrifice content quality for better visuals, or deliver excellent content with basic presentations that failed to engage students?

"What we need," one professor summarized, "is a way to transform our knowledge into visually compelling slides without having to become design professionals ourselves."

AI Tool Recommendation

Napkin.ai is an exceptional tool to create visually engaging slides without design expertise. What sets Napkin.ai apart is its ability to automatically transform complex textual content into professional visuals within seconds. Napkin.ai also offers extensive customization options, allowing users to tweak colours, fonts, layouts and even add icons to align visuals with their teaching style or institutional branding. Its intuitive interface ensures that even non-designers can produce high-quality visuals quickly, reducing preparation time while maintaining academic rigour.

How to Use Napkin.ai

1. **Sign Up or Log In:** Visit napkin.ai and create an account, or log in if you already have one.
2. **Create a New Napkin:** Click on "Create New Napkin" to start a new project.
3. **Input Your Content:** Paste or type your textual content into the provided space.

4. **Generate Visuals:** Click the "Spark" icon to automatically transform your text into visuals.napkin.ai.
5. **Customize as Needed:** Use the editing tools to adjust layouts, colours and styles to fit your preferences.
6. **Export or Share:** Once finalized, export your visuals in formats like PNG, SVG or PDF, or share them directly via a link.

How to Keep Your Data Safe

- **Leverage Local Export Options:** Export visuals as offline files (e.g. PNG or PDF) instead of sharing links to ensure sensitive academic content remains private and inaccessible online.
- **Consider Deleting Visuals:** Napkin.ai normally stores the visuals in the library after they are created. If any sensitive information is used, consider deleting the related visuals from library.

Smart Ways to Review AI Output

- **Cross-Check Visual Logic with Domain Expertise:** After generating visuals, verify if the structure aligns with your subject-matter knowledge. This ensures that the AI output accurately represents complex academic concepts without oversimplification.
- **Iterative Refinement:** Share initial drafts of visuals with the intended recipients during lectures and gather feedback on clarity and engagement.

Outcome

By integrating Napkin.ai into their workflow, professors significantly reduced the time spent on slide design while enhancing the clarity and engagement of their presentations. Instead of struggling with complex design tools, they could now transform their expertise into visually compelling slides in seconds. This allowed them to focus on delivering high-quality content without sacrificing visual appeal, ensuring that students grasped intricate concepts more effectively. What was once a time-consuming frustration became an effortless process, enabling educators to maintain academic rigour while keeping their classes visually engaging and dynamic.

Tailored Communication and Presentations

A strong presentation doesn't just involve making eye-catching slides; it actually hinges on persuasion. Whether you're pitching to investors, leading a team meeting or addressing a conference audience, how you structure and deliver your message determines its impact. Yet, crafting a compelling presentation is no small feat. It requires storytelling, visual design and data-driven insights, all of which must be uplifted by clarity and engagement. In the past (and even today), this process has involved manually designing slides, refining key points and rehearsing delivery.

But AI is changing the way professionals prepare and present. It can suggest data visualizations, optimize slide layouts and even generate speaker notes that align with your communication style. AI isn't replacing presenters; it's elevating them. But what does this transformation look like in real business settings? Let's explore how AI is helping teams create more effective presentations.

From Executive Boardrooms to Hospital Hallways

During one of our AI bootcamp discussions, a healthcare leader shared a presentation challenge that we have seen play out in many corporate settings.

A senior doctor who leads a regional hospital network mentioned a recurring communication challenge during our last healthcare management module. He was preparing a crucial presentation on a new patient-care initiative for two very different audiences: the hospital's Board of Directors and a town hall with the entire hospital staff scheduled for the following day.

The content for both presentations was essentially the same – progress updates, patient satisfaction statistics and upcoming procedural changes – but the communication needs differed dramatically. The board expected executive-level strategy and comprehensive data analysis, while nurses and support staff needed to understand the daily impact and practical implementation details.

In the past, he would create a dense, data-heavy slide deck for the board and then attempt to simplify it for staff, typically ending up with inconsistent messaging or spending countless hours redesigning everything.

> **AI Tool Recommendation**
>
> **Gamma.app** is a cutting-edge AI-powered presentation tool that simplifies the process of creating professional, engaging presentations tailored to diverse audiences. What makes Gamma.app unique is its ability to transform raw content into polished slide decks with minimal effort. Its standout features include "nested cards" for drilling into details, one-click design restyling and the ability to seamlessly import documents or presentations for AI-enhanced refinement. Moreover, Gamma.app's versatility in creating various content formats, including documents and websites, makes it an invaluable tool for professionals aiming to deliver consistent and impactful messaging across different platforms. Gamma.app empowers users to focus on their message rather than design complexities.

How to Use Gamma.app

First Iteration: Creating a Board Presentation
1. **Select/Add a Template Theme:** Start by choosing or adding a professional theme from Gamma's library that matches your presentation's tone (e.g. executive strategy).
2. **Input Content:** Paste your document or outline (e.g. patient-care initiative details) into Gamma.app.
3. **Generate Slides:** Use Gamma's AI to create an initial draft of the board presentation, focusing on strategic insights and comprehensive data analysis.
4. **Customize Design:** Refine the slides using Gamma's editor – adjust layouts, add visuals like graphs or charts and ensure alignment with your chosen theme.
5. **Export or Share:** Download the final presentation as a PowerPoint or PDF file, or share it securely via a link.

Second Iteration: Tailoring For Staff Audience

1. **Import Board Presentation:** Upload the finalized board presentation into Gamma.app as your starting point.
2. **Provide Detailed Instructions:** Specify what to include (e.g. practical implementation steps) and what to omit (e.g. detailed financial analysis). Highlight the need for simplified visuals and relatable examples tailored to staff roles.

3. **Generate Tailored Slides:** Let Gamma adapt the presentation based on your instructions, simplifying language and emphasizing daily impact over strategy.
4. **Review and Finalize:** Use Gamma's nested cards feature to drill down into specific slides and fine-tune them for clarity and engagement before sharing with staff.

How to Keep Your Data Safe (Gamma.app-Specific Suggestions)

- Pro users can **password-protect presentations** before sharing them via links. This ensures that only authorized individuals with the password can access sensitive content like patient statistics or procedural updates.
- **Use workspace settings to control who can view or edit presentations.** For example, set decks to "view-only" or limit editing rights to specific team members.
- When working on confidential projects, **disable auto-save features in settings** to prevent drafts from being stored on Gamma's servers unnecessarily.

Smart Ways to Review AI Output

1. After generating the initial presentation, **review each slide through the lens of your target audience** (e.g. board vs. staff). Ask whether each slide addresses their specific concerns – strategy for executives versus daily impact for staff – and refine accordingly.

2. **Share drafts with small focus groups (e.g. senior nurses or department heads) before finalizing them.** Use their feedback to identify gaps in clarity or relevance and adjust both messaging and visuals iteratively for maximum impact across audiences.

Outcome

By leveraging Gamma.app, the hospital leader streamlined the process of tailoring presentations for different audiences without compromising clarity or consistency. Instead of manually redesigning slides and risking messaging misalignment, he could quickly generate a board-level strategic presentation and seamlessly adapt it for staff with AI-driven refinements. This not only saved valuable preparation time but also ensured that both the Board and frontline healthcare workers received content relevant to their roles.

Email and Messaging

Every email you send carries weight. A well-crafted message can foster collaboration, influence decisions and strengthen relationships. But writing clear, professional and impactful emails isn't always easy – especially when time is limited.

For years, professionals have relied on templates, proofreading tools and manual revisions to refine their messaging. The challenge? Ensuring every email strikes the right tone, conveys intent effectively and gets the desired response – all without spending too much time on drafting.

AI-powered writing tools are transforming email communication. From refining tone and structure to summarizing lengthy conversations, AI helps professionals write better and faster. But how exactly does this impact day-to-day workflows? Let's explore how organizations are using AI to enhance business communication.

Navigating the Email Tsunami

During our AI bootcamp with a senior-care organization, their technology director shared a persistent challenge that many executives in the room found all too familiar. Each morning, he would start his day buried under an avalanche of emails.

Managing teams across multiple care facilities means that overnight, his inbox fills with lengthy updates, family inquiries and staff requests. By 9 a.m., he already feels like he's falling behind, struggling to separate urgent matters from routine updates.

During a leadership meeting, the CEO joked, "Have you cloned yourself yet to handle all that email?" The room chuckled, but the reality was far from funny. Sorting through the endless stream of messages was leaving him with little time to focus on bigger priorities – initiatives that could actually improve care quality across their facilities.

The real challenge remained: how could he keep up with the flood of emails without losing sight of the work that truly mattered?

AI Tool Recommendation

Microsoft Copilot is an AI-powered assistant to tackle the challenge of managing an overwhelming email inbox. Integrated within Microsoft 365 apps like Outlook, Copilot offers unique features such as "Prioritize My Inbox", which automatically categorizes and summarizes emails based on urgency and importance. It can also be "taught" to recognize specific topics, keywords or senders, ensuring that high-priority messages are flagged for immediate attention. Additionally, Copilot can draft email responses with customizable tone and length, saving time while maintaining professionalism. These capabilities allow executives to focus on strategic priorities without getting bogged down by routine email management.

Intermediate AI Literacy: WRITES

How to Use Microsoft Copilot

1. **Activate Copilot in Outlook:** Ensure Microsoft Copilot is enabled in your Outlook settings (available for Microsoft 365 subscribers).
2. **Teach Copilot Your Priorities:** Use the "Teach Copilot" feature to identify key topics, keywords (e.g. "urgent", "family inquiry"), and important senders (e.g. department heads, CEO). This helps Copilot prioritize relevant emails.
3. **Use the "Prioritize My Inbox" Feature:** Let Copilot summarize your inbox by grouping emails into categories such as "Urgent", "Action Required" and "Routine Updates". It will highlight critical messages first.
4. **Draft Responses Efficiently:** For emails requiring replies, use Copilot to draft responses. You can adjust tone and length with simple prompts like "Make it concise" or "Add a formal tone."
5. **Schedule a Daily Summary:** Ask Copilot to generate a daily summary of unread emails with actionable insights so you can address key issues without opening every message.

How to Keep Your Data Safe

- Microsoft Copilot operates within the Microsoft 365 service boundary, **ensuring that all data remains**

encrypted and secure within your organization's ecosystem. Sensitive emails and prompts are not used for training AI models or shared externally.
- **Restrict who in your organization can access Copilot's features** by configuring permissions through the Microsoft 365 Admin Center, ensuring only authorized users can interact with sensitive data.
- **Set up conditional access policies** in Azure Active Directory to ensure that only devices meeting security criteria (e.g. encrypted or compliant devices) can access Copilot features.

Smart Ways to Review AI Output

1. **Contextual Validation of Summaries:** After using the "Prioritize My Inbox" feature, cross-check summaries against original emails for critical nuances like tone or context that might be misinterpreted by AI. This ensures no important details are overlooked in high-stakes communications.
2. **Iterative Refinement with Feedback Loops:** Regularly provide feedback to Copilot on its prioritization and draft responses using built-in feedback tools (e.g. thumbs up/down). Over time, this improves its ability to align outputs with your preferences and organizational needs.

3. **Simulate Scenarios for Testing Accuracy:** Periodically test Copilot by feeding it sample inbox scenarios (e.g. mock urgent updates) and reviewing how well it categorizes and prioritizes them. This helps ensure its performance remains reliable under varying workloads.

Outcome

By integrating Microsoft Copilot into his workflow, the technology director transformed email management from an overwhelming burden into a streamlined, efficient process. Instead of spending hours sifting through messages, Copilot prioritized urgent emails, summarized lengthy threads and even drafted responses, freeing up valuable time for strategic initiatives. With AI handling the routine clutter, he could focus on improving care quality across facilities rather than staying buried in his inbox.

Speaking and Collaboration

The spoken word has always carried unique power – it conveys not just information but emotion, urgency and human connection. Yet, for most organizations, speech remains underutilized as a medium, limited by the traditional constraints of production costs, technical complexity and distribution challenges.

Leaders across industries struggle with a fundamental communication challenge: effectively translating complex expertise into clear, engaging dialogue that maintains both technical accuracy and audience connection. Whether addressing media, stakeholders or colleagues, conventional preparation methods like static-briefing documents and rehearsed talking points simply cannot adapt to the nuanced demands of modern communication exchanges.

AI is bridging this divide by serving as an intelligent dialogue partner, helping professionals practise, refine and master messaging across contexts. Organizations implementing these voice collaboration technologies are developing more dynamic communication skills, enabling clearer explanations of technical concepts, more adaptable responses to unexpected questions and ultimately stronger connections with diverse audiences – as the following example will demonstrate.

Mastering the Art of Expert Media Dialogue

While hosting an AI bootcamp for a leading sleep-and-wellness company, the CEO shared a situation that struck a chord. With over two decades of leadership experience and countless media interactions under his belt, he had always prided himself on being the company's most effective spokesperson. But the landscape was shifting beneath his feet.

Intermediate AI Literacy: WRITES

Sleep science was no longer just about comfortable mattresses; it had evolved into a complex intersection of neuroscience, AI-driven technology and personalized wellness. Every media interaction now came loaded with technical questions about sleep algorithms, biometric sensors and circadian rhythm optimization. While he understood his company's innovations deeply, translating this complexity into compelling, quotable insights for different audiences was becoming a constant challenge.

The stakes were particularly high. A single oversimplified explanation could undermine their positioning as a technology leader. Too technical a response could lose the audience entirely. The traditional approach of reviewing briefing documents and doing quick practice sessions with his communications team wasn't cutting it anymore. He needed a way to master this new narrative - one that could position him as both a visionary business leader and a credible voice in the technological transformation of sleep science.

What he needed was an intelligent sparring partner – one that could help him practise different ways of explaining complex topics, challenge his responses and refine his message until it struck the perfect balance between technical accuracy and engaging storytelling.

> ### AI Tool Recommendation
>
> To address this communication challenge, integrating **ChatGPT's Advanced Voice Mode** into the CEO's preparation process would be highly beneficial. This feature enables natural, real-time conversations, allowing users to practise articulating complex concepts and receive immediate feedback. By engaging in simulated press interactions, the CEO can refine his messaging, ensuring clarity and resonance with diverse audiences.

How to Use ChatGPT Advanced Voice Mode

1. **Set Up ChatGPT with Advanced Voice Mode:**
   - Ensure the latest version of the ChatGPT app is installed on the CEO's device.
   - Activate the Advanced Voice Mode feature within the app settings.
2. **Upload Relevant Materials:**
   - Input key briefing documents, technical papers and recent articles on sleep technology and wellness trends into ChatGPT to provide context.
3. **Simulate Press Interactions:**
   - Engage in voice-based conversations with ChatGPT, posing potential media questions to the AI.
   - Practise responding to these questions, focusing on clarity and coherence.

4. **Receive Feedback and Refine Responses:**
   - Utilize ChatGPT's feedback to identify areas for improvement in messaging.
   - Iterate on responses to enhance delivery and impact.
5. **Develop Compelling Narratives:**
   - Collaborate with ChatGPT to craft stories that effectively communicate the company's innovations in sleep technology and their benefits to consumers.

How to Keep Your Data Safe

- **Go to ChatGPT settings and turn off "Include your audio recordings" and "Improve the model for everyone" under data controls.** This ensures that your voice conversations are not used to train OpenAI models, keeping your data private.
- **Disable the "Background conversations" feature in settings.** This prevents accidental recording of sensitive discussions while multitasking or using other apps.
- **Periodically delete sensitive conversations from your chat history.** OpenAI retains transcripts of voice chats, so clearing them ensures no residual data is stored unnecessarily.
- **Do not disclose confidential company data, financial figures or unreleased strategic plans during the simulation. Use placeholder data or generic examples instead.

Smart Ways to Review AI Output

- Compare ChatGPT's suggestions on your responses with official company messaging and advice from human communication experts (PR team). **Cross-reference suggestions for accuracy.**
- Look out for generic advice or feedback that misunderstands the nuanced context of your industry or specific situation. **Proactively assess feedback quality.**
- Evaluate if the AI-generated **media questions feel like plausible challenges** based on the context provided.
- Is the feedback suitable for the specific type of media interaction being practiced (e.g., critical interview vs. friendly chat)? **Ensure to evaluate contextual relevance**
- If AI advice is unclear (e.g., "be more persuasive"), prompt it for specific examples or alternative phrasings. **Actively seek clarification on vague feedback.**

Outcome

By integrating ChatGPT's Advanced Voice Mode into his media preparation, the CEO gained a dynamic, AI-driven sparring partner that helped him refine complex messaging with precision. Instead of relying solely on briefing documents or last-minute rehearsals, he could now engage in real-time simulations, practising responses to tough media questions and fine-tuning his delivery. What was once a high-stakes challenge became an opportunity to position himself as a credible, articulate leader at the forefront of sleep technology.

Neat Tricks

How to Use Voice AI Effectively

1. Voice Interaction Best Practices

Do:
- Speak in complete sentences (e.g. "Summarize today's meeting notes about Q2 goals" vs. "Summarize notes").
- Pause strategically: Let the AI process before continuing.
- Correct mid-stream: Interrupt ChatGPT.
- Voice with phrases like "Wait, I meant..."

Don't:
- Ramble without structure (as it helps prevent misinterpretation).
- Assume the AI remembers context beyond three–four exchanges.

2. Technical Optimization

Do:
- Add punctuation mentally: Think "period" or "comma" to guide intonation.

- Use wake-word reset: Say "New topic" to clear prior context.
- Adjust speed: Slow down for complex queries (e.g. "Break down Kant's categorical imperative...").

Don't
- Speak in noisy environments without noise-cancelling.
- Use slang/idioms/abbreviations without clarification ("BS" → "Bullseye report").

3. **Learning and Productivity Hacks**

Do:
- Frame prompts as collaborations: "Let's brainstorm five ways to reduce project delays."
- Leverage follow-ups: "Expand point three with real-world examples."

Don't:
- Use vague requests like "Help me learn"; instead, specify "Create a 10-minute lesson on Python loops."

4. **Ethical and Safety Considerations**

Do:
- Anonymize sensitive data: Avoid sharing personal IDs/addresses.

Intermediate AI Literacy: WRITES

- Verify critical outputs: Cross-check medical/legal advice.

Don't
- Assume emotional reciprocity (e.g. "You're my friend" risks over-reliance).

This chapter was written with the help of ChatGPT 4o Canvas and Perplexity.ai.

8

Advanced AI Literacy: ADDS

"If we have data, let's look at data. If all we have are opinions, let's go with mine."

— JIM BARKSDALE

The Abacus: Humanity's First Step Towards Computational Thinking

Picture a merchant in ancient times, his fingers dancing across a simple wooden frame strung with beads. With quick, practised movements, he completes complex calculations that would otherwise take several minutes of mental effort. This humble device – the abacus – represents one of humanity's earliest and most profound technological breakthroughs in extending our cognitive capabilities.

Before electronic calculators and digital computers, the abacus stood as humanity's primary computational aid for nearly 4,000 years. More than a mere counting tool, it was an external memory device, a physical embodiment of abstract numerical concepts and perhaps arguably, the first widespread technology to augment human thinking. The abacus didn't just help people calculate – it fundamentally changed *how* they thought about calculation.

The impact of this seemingly simple tool was far-reaching, shaping not just arithmetic but also the way people approached problem-solving and computation in the following ways:

- **Cognitive Amplification:** The abacus extended mental capacity, allowing users to work with numbers far beyond what working memory alone could handle.
- **Algorithmic Thinking:** Each calculation on an abacus follows a set procedure – an algorithm – teaching users to break complex problems into discrete, manageable steps. This procedural thinking laid the conceptual groundwork for modern computation.
- **Democratized Expertise:** While written mathematical notation remained accessible only to the educated few, the abacus provided a tactile, intuitive interface that made sophisticated calculation available to a much broader population. A skilled abacus user could perform additions and multiplications of large numbers with speed that would astonish modern observers.

In the centuries that followed, mechanical calculators, electronic computers and eventually digital technology continued this trajectory of computational amplification. Each innovation built upon the fundamental insight embodied by the abacus: that human cognition could be extended through external tools specifically designed to handle certain types of thinking.

AI: The New Arithmetic of the Digital Age

Today, artificial intelligence represents not just an incremental improvement in our computational tools, but a fundamental shift in our relationship with information processing – one that parallels the revolutionary impact of the abacus, but at an unprecedented scale and pace.

Consider the words of mathematician and philosopher Alfred North Whitehead, who in his 1911 book, *An Introduction to Mathematics*, observed[1]:

"Civilization advances by extending the number of important operations which we can perform without thinking about them."

The abacus allowed merchants to trade without mentally tracking every calculation. Modern AI allows us to process, analyse and derive insights from volumes of data that would otherwise be humanly impossible to manage.

Just as the abacus transformed who could calculate and what could be calculated, AI is now transforming who can analyse complex information and what kinds of problems can be solved successfully. A customer service manager can easily analyse thousands of support

---

[1] Whitehead, Alfred North. 2015. Persuasion Blog." Healthyinfluence. https://tinyurl.com/2tb26d4h.

tickets to identify sentiment trends and emerging issues. A small business owner can perform market analysis and automate inventory management once reserved for corporations with dedicated departments. A social media coordinator can analyse audience engagement patterns across platforms and automate content scheduling, optimizing reach without advanced analytical training. These capabilities – analysing vast datasets, interpreting human sentiments and automating routine processes – are becoming accessible to everyone, not just specialists.

This democratization of analytical capability isn't just changing how we work – it's transforming how we think.

The ADDS Framework: Expanding Analytical Capabilities with AI

On that note, we introduce the ADDS framework that offers a structured approach to leveraging AI's analytical capabilities across four key dimensions:

1. **Automate Core Processes**
    - AI streamlines repetitive tasks like report generation, scheduling and document management, freeing up cognitive bandwidth for strategic work. By handling routine processes, AI enables professionals to focus on creativity, decision-making and high-impact initiatives.

2. **Decode Markets and Competition**
   - AI continuously tracks competitor moves, market trends and industry sentiment, turning scattered data into real-time strategic insights. This shifts market intelligence from occasional research to a persistent, data-driven advantage.

3. **Data-Driven Decision Making**
   - AI transforms raw data into actionable intelligence by identifying patterns, correlations and anomalies. It enhances decision-making by providing objective, scalable analysis, allowing professionals to focus on strategic implications rather than manual data processing.

4. **Stakeholder Sentiment Analysis**
   - AI quantifies sentiment from customer reviews, employee feedback and social media, offering a real-time pulse on stakeholder perceptions. This turns relationship management into a data-informed practice, helping businesses proactively address concerns and opportunities.

Together, these four dimensions extend your analytical capabilities, enabling smarter automation, sharper market awareness and more informed decision-making. The following sections will explore practical tools and techniques to implement each component in our daily work.

Automate Core Processes

Think about your typical workday. How much of it is spent on tasks that, while necessary, don't truly require your unique skills or strategic thinking? Scheduling meetings, generating routine reports, organizing files, processing standard requests – the list goes on. These are the essential but often repetitive cogs that keep the organizational machine running. The problem isn't just the time these tasks consume; it's the cognitive drain. Every minute you spend on low-level administrative work is a minute you're *not* focused on innovation, problem-solving or high-impact decisions. It's like a Formula 1 car stuck in city traffic – all that potential horsepower wasted on stop-and-go movement. That's where AI-driven automation is transforming the workplace. In our opinion, it's not here to replace humans; rather, it will only help liberate them. By intelligently handling routine processes, AI frees up your cognitive bandwidth, allowing you to focus on the strategic, creative and interpersonal aspects of your role that truly drive value. It's about shifting from being bogged down in the mundane to being empowered to lead and innovate.

But what does this look like in reality? How can AI help an organization free up critical bandwidth that can improve outcomes? Time to explore another example.

The Hidden Cost of Investment Research

During an executive AI bootcamp, we met the head of corporate strategy at a mid-sized investment bank. He looked exhausted. When we asked about his challenges, he shared a story that struck a chord with many in the room.

Every quarter, his team scrambled to research potential acquisition targets, summarize investor presentations and analyse earnings call transcripts. The workload spiked before strategic planning meetings, with analysts manually extracting key insights from dense financial documents and disparate data sources.

"These are some of our sharpest minds, but they spend days sifting through reports instead of generating investment ideas," he admitted. "By the time we get to strategy discussions, they're too drained to think critically. The real cost isn't just the time – it's the insights we never get to because everyone is stuck in information-processing mode."

The frustrating part? The process was highly structured. Analysts followed a predictable workflow, yet they remained bogged down in repetitive, manual tasks that added little strategic value.

What he needed was a solution that didn't just automate document analysis but preserved the firm's expertise – helping analysts move beyond data extraction to high-value investment decision-making.

Advanced AI Literacy: ADDS

> ### AI Tool Recommendation: Claude Projects
>
> **Claude Projects** would be ideal for this investment research scenario. Unlike traditional workflows requiring manual extraction from multiple documents, Claude Projects allows the investment bank to create a structured workspace where teams can collaborate on analysing financial documents. With its 200k context window (equivalent to a 500-page book), analysts can upload all relevant financial reports, presentations and transcripts into a single organized environment.
>
> Claude Projects excels at maintaining context across multiple documents and conversations over time, critical for quarter-to-quarter comparison and trend analysis. Its ability to understand financial terminology and maintain a persistent memory of previous analyses makes it uniquely suited for investment research that requires both breadth of document processing and depth of financial insight.

How to Setup and Use Claude Projects

1. **Creating a Project:**
   - Log into Claude.ai with a Pro or Team account
   - Click on "New Project" from below the prompt box
   - Name your project (e.g. "Q1 2025 Acquisition Targets")

- Add a description to clarify the project's purpose (e.g. "Analysis of potential fintech acquisition targets for Q1 2025 strategic planning")
2. **Setting Custom Instructions:**
    - Navigate to the project settings
    - Add detailed custom instructions, such as:
    You are an expert financial analyst assisting our investment banking team with acquisition target research.
    When analysing financial documents:
    – Focus on companies with consistent revenue growth above 15 per cent year-over-year
    – Flag any debt-to-EBITDA ratios exceeding 3.5x as high risk
    – Pay special attention to recurring revenue streams and customer retention metrics
    – Identify synergies with our existing portfolio companies in financial services
    – Highlight management teams with proven M&A integration experience
    – Use standard financial terminology and ratios common in investment banking
    – Present financial data in tables with consistent formatting
    – Always calculate year-over-year and quarter-over-quarter percentage changes
    – When uncertain about financial data, highlight the ambiguity rather than making assumptions

- Format executive summaries with bullet points for key metrics followed by two to three paragraphs of strategic analysis

While configuring projects, custom instructions allow users to set up user-defined guidelines or constraints that shape the model's behavior, responses or outputs.

3. **Document Management:**
   - Supported formats include PDFs, text files, spreadsheets and more
   - Organize documents by target company or document type
   - Use consistent naming conventions (e.g., "CompanyName_Q1_2025_Earnings.pdf")
   - Consider creating a document inventory at the start of the project to track what's been uploaded.

Suggested Prompt

I need you to analyse the financial documents I've uploaded to this project for our potential acquisition targets. Based on these documents, please provide:

1. **Comprehensive Financial Analysis:**
   - Create a detailed financial health assessment for each target company
   - Calculate key ratios including profit margins, Return on Equity (ROE), Return on Assets (ROA) and debt-servicing capacity

- Identify growth trends in revenue, Earnings Before Interest, Taxes, Depreciation and Amortization (EBITDA) and net income over the past 8 quarters
- Assess cash flow stability and capital allocation strategies
- Evaluate balance sheet strength and liquidity positions

2. **Strategic Insights:**
   - Extract stated strategic priorities from management statements
   - Identify key investment areas and R&D focus
   - Analyse competitive positioning statements and market share claims
   - Evaluate the company's digital transformation initiatives
   - Assess geographic expansion plans and market penetration strategies

3. **Risk Assessment:**
   - Identify regulatory challenges mentioned in disclosures
   - Highlight pending litigation or compliance issues
   - Analyse customer concentration risks
   - Evaluate technology obsolescence threats
   - Assess leadership transition risks and key person dependencies

4. **Acquisition Suitability:**
   - Evaluate cultural alignment based on stated corporate values

Advanced AI Literacy: ADDS

- Identify potential integration challenges
- Assess overlapping customer bases and product cannibalization risks
- Calculate potential synergies in operations, technology and market reach
- Provide a preliminary valuation range based on comparable transactions

Please format your analysis as an executive summary with supporting detailed sections. Include visual representations of key metrics where appropriate, and highlight areas where you believe additional information would strengthen the analysis.

Prompting Best Practices Used

1. **Clear Analysis Parameters:** The prompt explicitly defines what financial metrics and qualitative information to extract, ensuring Claude focuses on relevant information.
2. **Output Structure Specification:** The prompt clearly defines what the final outputs should look like, including the organization of insights for executive consumption.
3. **Knowledge Continuity:** The prompt emphasizes the need to maintain insights over time, leveraging Claude Projects' persistent memory capabilities.
4. **Task Decomposition:** The prompt breaks down the complex research task into specific components, making it easier for Claude to process systematically.

5. **Analytical Depth Guidance:** The prompt specifies the level of detail required for each analysis area, ensuring Claude provides sufficiently comprehensive insights.

How to Keep Your Data Safe

- Choose which conversations and insights to share with the broader team, keeping sensitive analyses private when necessary. **Practice selective sharing.**
- **Claude does not store or use your conversations for model training by default,** providing an additional layer of data security without requiring any special settings.
- Create separate projects for highly confidential acquisition targets to **isolate sensitive information**.
- Only upload the documents that are necessary for the analysis, avoiding the inclusion of unnecessary sensitive information.
- **Consider deleting sensitive documents** or entire conversations within the Project after analysis is complete and findings are secured externally.

Smart Ways to Review AI Output

- **Compare key figures,** ratios and summaries generated by Claude against the original source documents.
- **Identify and investigate AI outputs** inconsistent with established analytical expectations or prior findings.

- Verify that **Claude's interpretations align with the specific investment criteria** defined in project custom instructions.
- **Prompt Claude for specific data points** or document excerpts if its output provides only general statements on risk or opportunity.
- **Maintain clear records** (e.g., project notes, external logs) documenting verification, corrections and reviewer rationale for AI insights.

Outcome

By integrating Claude Projects into their research workflow, the investment bank significantly reduced the time spent on manual data extraction while improving the depth and accuracy of their financial analysis. Analysts could now upload vast amounts of financial reports, earnings call transcripts and investor presentations into a single, structured workspace, allowing them to extract insights and track trends effortlessly. Instead of being bogged down by repetitive tasks, the team could focus on high-value investment decision-making, leading to sharper strategic insights and more effective deal evaluations.

Decode Markets and Competition

Picture this: you're in a strategy session, and someone asks, "What are our competitors up to?" The room falls silent. You have the last quarter's market report, a few vague updates from the sales team and a gut feeling based on industry chatter – but no one has the full picture. Meanwhile, the market is shifting, and competitors are already adapting to trends you haven't even spotted.

In today's hyper-connected world, competitive advantage isn't just about making smarter moves; it's also about making them faster. Yet, many organizations still rely on periodic competitive analyses, quarterly market reviews and annual strategy refreshes. The problem? This slow, episodic approach creates blind spots in a business landscape where disruption happens in real time.

Traditionally, companies assign teams to manually collect competitor insights, analyse scattered data and compile detailed reports. But by the time those reports reach decision-makers, they're often outdated. This lag leaves companies reacting to changes instead of anticipating them.

AI is revolutionizing this by turning market intelligence into a continuous, real-time strategic radar. It tracks competitor moves, customer sentiment and emerging trends across vast data sources – transforming market awareness from a periodic snapshot into an always-on advantage. This isn't just about speed; it's a fundamental shift in how organizations stay ahead.

So how are businesses using AI to gain an edge? What does continuous market intelligence look like in practice? Let's examine a revealing case.

The Invisible Market Disruption

At an executive AI bootcamp, a CEO of an industrial equipment manufacturer shared a painful lesson over coffee. His company, a market leader for over 70 years, had just lost three major contracts in Asia – to a competitor they had barely considered a threat.

Despite investing heavily in traditional market intelligence – quarterly reports, trade shows and competitor tracking – the company missed the rise of a mid-sized European manufacturer. This emerging player didn't make splashy announcements or aggressive marketing moves. Instead, they built influence through technical webinars, niche engineering forums and partnerships with sustainability consultants who shaped buying decisions. By the time the competitor appeared in conventional market reports, they had already positioned themselves as leaders in sustainable processing technology – exactly what customers were prioritizing.

The real issue wasn't just overlooking a competitor; it was the limitations of episodic market research in an always-evolving landscape. Quarterly intelligence cycles left blind spots, allowing disruptive trends to go unnoticed until they became impossible to ignore. Tracking fragmented market signals across technical forums, global discussions and emerging partnerships was beyond what their traditional methods could handle.

What the CEO needed was continuous, AI-powered market intelligence – a system that could monitor real-time industry conversations, detect emerging technology trends and synthesize scattered signals into actionable insights. Without this shift, he knew his team would keep playing catch-up in an industry where the real competitive battles were being fought in spaces they weren't even watching.

AI Tools Recommendation

For addressing the challenge of continuous market research and staying ahead of competitors in an evolving landscape, **Perplexity AI** combined with **Perplexity Spaces** offers a robust solution. Here's why:

- **Continuous Market Intelligence**: Perplexity AI provides real-time updates and insights, crucial for tracking emerging trends and competitor activities. This capability helps mitigate the limitations of episodic market research by ensuring that teams stay informed about the latest developments in their industry.

- **Organized Collaboration:** Perplexity Spaces allows teams to organize research threads and files by topic or project, creating a centralized hub for market intelligence. This feature is particularly valuable for continuous market research as it enables teams to maintain a structured approach to monitoring industry conversations, technical forums and partnerships. Spaces facilitate collaboration among team members, ensuring that insights are shared effectively and that everyone is aligned with the latest market developments.
- **Customization and Security:** Within Spaces, teams can customize AI assistants to focus on specific market segments or competitors, enhancing the relevance of the insights generated. Additionally, Spaces provides robust access controls, ensuring that sensitive market research data remains secure during collaborative efforts.

How to Use Perplexity Spaces for Continuous Market Research

To effectively utilize Perplexity Spaces for continuous market research:

- **Create Dedicated Spaces:** Set up separate Spaces for different market segments or competitors to keep research organized and focused.

- **Upload Relevant Files**: Include internal reports, competitor analyses and industry publications in Spaces to integrate both internal and external data sources.
- **Conduct Deep Research**: Use Perplexity's Deep Research feature to generate comprehensive reports on emerging trends and competitor strategies, saving time and enhancing the depth of analysis.
- **Collaborate and Analyse**: Regularly review and discuss findings with team members within Spaces, ensuring that insights are actionable and aligned with business strategies.

Suggested Prompts

- Create a comprehensive report within this Space on the current landscape of sustainable processing technology in Asia. Include an analysis of recent partnerships between manufacturers and sustainability consultants, and highlight any emerging trends or technologies that could disrupt the market.
- Develop a dashboard within this Space to track real-time mentions of our competitors in technical forums and niche engineering discussions. Provide weekly summaries of key insights and identify any shifts in market sentiment towards our products.
- Analyse all files uploaded to this Space related to competitor strategies in sustainable processing technology and identify gaps in our current market approach.

Advanced AI Literacy: ADDS

- Provide recommendations for how we can improve our competitive positioning based on these insights.
- Map the influence networks within this Space by analysing the interactions between key industry influencers, sustainability consultants and manufacturers. Identify potential partners or collaborators who could enhance our market presence.

How to Keep Your Data Safe

Perplexity Spaces offers robust safety features to protect your data:

- Manage who can view or edit your research and files within each Space, ensuring only authorized team members have access. **Have necessary access controls.**
- For **Enterprise Pro users, all files and searches are excluded from AI training** by default, safeguarding sensitive data.
- Spaces allows for secure collaboration by providing a controlled environment where sensitive information can be shared without compromising data integrity.

Smart Ways to Review AI Output

- **Compare Perplexity's findings** about competitor activities with information from your trusted industry contacts and internal market reports to verify accuracy.
- **Look for inconsistencies** between Perplexity's market trend analysis and your company's direct experience

in the field, which may indicate areas needing deeper investigation.
- **Identify generic statements about market trends** and request more specific evidence or examples from particular technical forums.
- **Implement a feedback loop** where AI outputs are continuously reviewed and refined based on new market data and team feedback, ensuring insights remain relevant and actionable.

Outcome

By adopting Perplexity AI and Perplexity Spaces, the company transformed its market intelligence approach from reactive to proactive. Instead of relying on delayed quarterly reports, they could now continuously track emerging competitors, sustainability trends and key industry discussions in real time. With structured Spaces for focused research and AI-driven deep analysis, the team identified market shifts early – allowing them to respond strategically rather than playing catch-up. What was once a blind spot became a competitive advantage, ensuring they stayed ahead in an industry where disruptions often happen long before they appear in traditional reports.

Data-Driven Decision Making

Consider the last major business decision your team faced – whether to enter a new market, adjust pricing or allocate resources to a strategic initiative. How much of that decision was based on clear, objective data and how much relied on gut instinct or incomplete reports? In many organizations, decision-making feels like navigating through fog – you have data, but without the right tools to interpret it, you're still guessing.

The problem isn't a lack of information; it's the challenge of extracting meaningful insights from an overwhelming volume of sales figures, customer interactions, market trends and operational metrics. Raw data, on its own, is like a massive puzzle with no clear way to assemble the pieces into a useful picture. Misinterpreting or overlooking key patterns can lead to costly missteps.

AI is changing this by transforming raw data into actionable intelligence. It doesn't just generate reports; it detects hidden correlations, anomalies and predictive signals that would be impossible to spot manually. With AI, leaders can quickly analyse vast datasets to uncover the root causes of problems, anticipate shifts in demand and identify untapped opportunities.

But how does this work in real-world business scenarios? How can leaders without technical expertise leverage AI for better decision-making? Let's explore a practical application.

The Hidden Deal Breaker

During an AI literacy bootcamp with a leading professional services firm, we connected with the head of Deal Advisory for their private equity practice. Over lunch, he recounted a cautionary tale that had fundamentally changed how his team approached financial due diligence.

"We recently advised a corporation on what looked like a straightforward acquisition," he explained, fatigue evident in his voice. "The target company showed steady growth, consistent margins, and all the standard metrics pointed to a solid investment. Six weeks into our process, just days before closing, our junior associate spotted an anomaly that nearly everyone had missed."

The story unfolded in painful detail. His team had received over five years of financial data across multiple Excel workbooks – thousands of rows spanning dozens of tabs with detailed sales figures, cost breakdowns and operational KPIs. They followed their standard due diligence playbook: senior analysts assigned specific areas to examine, junior team members processed the data into standardized templates and partners reviewed summary dashboards highlighting key trends.

"What we missed was a pattern of revenue recognition that only became visible when looking at daily sales data across multiple business units simultaneously," he admitted. "The company had been systematically shifting revenue between quarters to create the illusion of smooth growth – moving just enough each time to stay under our standard variance thresholds."

This wasn't a failure of expertise or diligence – it was a limitation of human cognitive capacity. The anomaly existed in the relationship between hundreds of data points spread across different files, timeframes and business segments. It wasn't visible in the aggregated reports or summary dashboards that formed the basis of their analysis. The pattern only emerged when the entire dataset was examined holistically, something practically impossible for human analysts constrained by time and cognitive limitations.

"We're dealing with increasingly sophisticated financial engineering," the practice leader continued. "The days when red flags waved themselves are long gone. Modern due diligence failures rarely come from missing obvious issues – they come from not connecting subtle patterns across massive datasets."

The Deal Advisory team needed a solution that could ingest years of complex financial data, systematically identify subtle patterns and anomalies that crossed traditional analysis boundaries, and elevate potential issues for expert human evaluation – all while maintaining the confidentiality standards essential to their practice.

AT Tool Recommendation

Include a mention of ChatGPT 4o for analytics strengths in a box, make prominent

ChatGPT-4o excels due to its capacity for complex reasoning and pattern recognition across vast datasets.

Unlike traditional statistical tools that require predefined parameters, ChatGPT can identify subtle anomalies and correlations that might be missed by conventional methods. ChatGPT 4o can perform the analysis in the following ways:
- **Reasoning about Data:** Use natural language prompts to ask questions about trends, correlations and outliers.
- **Pattern Recognition:** Identify non-obvious patterns across disparate datasets using advanced algorithms.
- **Holistic Analysis:** Analyse the entire dataset simultaneously, overcoming the limitations of human cognitive capacity.
- **Data Interpretation:** Provide human-readable summaries and insights from complex financial data.

Types of Data Analysis You Can Perform on Excel/CSV Files
- **Synthesis:** Combining or analysing information to create new insights
- **Transformation:** Reshaping information while preserving its essence
- **Extraction:** Pulling specific information from a dataset
- **Anomaly Detection:** Identifying unusual patterns or outliers in data
- **Anomaly Mitigation:** Fixing common anomalies identified

> - **Advanced Statistical Analysis:** Time series, correlation, regression analysis
> - **Interactive Dashboards:** Creating visual, interactive tools to explore data

How to Use ChatGPT-4o

Here's a breakdown of how to use ChatGPT-4o for specific analysis types:

Data Preparation:
- Upload all the files within the ChatGPT interface.

Transformation:
- Prompt: "Reshape the data to calculate daily sales for each business unit. Then, calculate the month-over-month revenue growth for each unit."

Extraction:
- Prompt: "Extract all transactions with sales exceeding $X (insert target's average sales)."

Anomaly Detection:
- Prompt: "Identify any unusual patterns in revenue recognition across different business units. Focus on instances where revenue appears to have been shifted between quarters."

Anomaly Mitigation:
- Prompt: "Based on the anomalies identified, highlight transactions that appear to have been adjusted to meet specific quarterly targets. Provide

a rationale for why these transactions are flagged as anomalies."

Advanced Statistical Analysis:
- Prompt: "Perform time series analysis on the daily sales data for each business unit. Look for correlations and regression analysis to identify any statistically significant relationships between different units or time periods. Specifically, flag any instances where a decrease in sales in one unit is offset by an increase in another unit in the same quarter."

Synthesis:
- Prompt: "Synthesize the findings from the anomaly detection and statistical analysis. Provide a summary of the key patterns and anomalies that suggest revenue shifting. Explain how these patterns could impact the overall financial health and valuation of the company."

Interactive Dashboards:
- Prompt: "Create an interactive dashboard that allows me to explore the daily sales data, revenue growth rates and identified anomalies. Include filters for business units, time periods and anomaly types."

How to Keep Your Data Safe

- Navigate to ChatGPT's settings and **explicitly opt out of having your data used for training the model** to protect your confidential financial information.

Advanced AI Literacy: ADDS

- **Share only the minimal financial data** needed for each specific analysis rather than entire datasets.
- Before uploading financial files, **remove or mask identifying information** about acquisition targets when such details aren't essential for the analysis.
- Download and **securely store your analysis results**, then **clear conversation history** from ChatGPT after completing sensitive financial reviews.

Smart Ways to Review AI Output

1. **Look for discrepancies** between ChatGPT's statistical analysis and financial patterns your experienced analysts would expect to see in legitimate business operations.
2. Ensure ChatGPT's interpretation of financial data accounts for industry-specific accounting practices and business models **relevant** to the acquisition target.
3. **Identify any vague conclusions** about financial anomalies and request more precise quantitative evidence.
4. **Document each verification** step taken to validate ChatGPT's findings, especially when critical investment decisions depend on the analysis.
5. **Create scenario tests** involving known financial manipulations (like channel stuffing or expense shifting) to calibrate your team's confidence in ChatGPT's anomaly detection capabilities.

Outcome

By integrating ChatGPT-4o into their due diligence process, the Deal Advisory team gained the ability to detect subtle financial anomalies that traditional methods often missed. Instead of relying solely on manual reviews and standardized reports, they could now analyse entire datasets holistically, uncovering hidden revenue manipulation patterns across different timeframes and business units. This AI-powered approach not only saved valuable time but also strengthened risk assessments – ensuring no critical detail was overlooked. What was once a reactive, time-intensive process became a proactive, high-precision analysis, allowing the firm to safeguard investments with greater confidence.

Stakeholder Sentiment Analysis

It's 10 p.m., and you're preparing for tomorrow's all-hands meeting. The latest employee survey results are in, but they're a mixed bag – some praise, some frustration and a lot of noise in between. You need to address it, but how do you separate the signal from the static? Your customers are vocal too – reviews are piling up online, and social media is buzzing with opinions about your latest move. If only you had someone to bounce this off, someone to help you read the room – better still, the world – instantly, without waiting for a focus group.

Advanced AI Literacy: ADDS

This is the reality leaders face: stakeholders – employees, customers, partners – are louder and more connected than ever, but understanding their collective pulse feels like guesswork. Traditional methods like surveys or PR reports take time, and by the time you've arrived at answers, the conversation moves on. You need insight now, not next quarter.

That's where AI steps in as a game-changer. Imagine a tool that listens to every voice, distills the sentiment and hands you the clarity to act – all in real time. No scheduling, no bias, just pure insight. Let's explore how organizations are using AI to turn stakeholder chatter into strategic gold.

The Sentiment Blind Spot

During an executive AI literacy program, we spoke with the Chief Strategy Officer of a national retail chain with over 500 locations. As we discussed AI's role in customer intelligence, she shared a harsh lesson from the previous holiday season.

"Our best revenue quarter nearly destroyed our brand," she admitted. "While sales were soaring, frustration was quietly building – only we didn't see it until it exploded on social media."

The company relied on structured feedback mechanisms: post-purchase surveys, mystery shoppers and Net Promoter Score tracking. But these methods captured only a fraction of customer sentiment. What they missed was where the real frustration was surfacing: X and other online forums. Customers weren't filling out surveys; they were venting publicly about long lines, confusing checkout interfaces and overwhelmed employees. A viral post from a former employee detailing system flaws ignited a firestorm, drawing millions of views.

"By the time it hit our executive dashboard, the damage was done," she said. "What could have been a small fix turned into a PR crisis." The problem wasn't a lack of concern for customer experience – it was the gap between episodic feedback cycles and real-time sentiment shifts. Without a way to continuously track unstructured feedback across multiple channels, they had been caught off guard.

The CSO needed a solution that could monitor customer sentiment holistically, detect emerging frustrations before they escalated and distill actionable insights without drowning the team in noise.

AI Tools Recommendation

Grok is an ideal AI solution for addressing the sentiment blind spot faced by the national retail chain due to these reasons:

- **Real-Time Data Access**: Grok integrates directly with X (formerly Twitter); enabling real-time access to public sentiment data.

Advanced AI Literacy: ADDS

> - **Immediate Customer Insights:** It instantly analyses customer feedback, emerging trends and potential PR issues as they develop.
> - **Comprehensive Sentiment View:** It processes vast amounts of unstructured data from X posts, comments and interactions. And provides a more holistic understanding of customer sentiment compared to traditional feedback methods.

Grok's ability to tap into the X ecosystem in real-time offers several advantages:

1. Immediate detection of emerging issues before they escalate
2. Access to authentic, unsolicited customer feedback
3. Ability to track sentiment across a broader customer base
4. Real-time monitoring of viral posts or trending topics related to the brand

This approach allows the company to stay ahead of potential PR crises and address customer concerns proactively, rather than reactively.

How to Use Grok to Analyse Customer Dissatisfaction

- **Set up Monitoring Parameters:**
Prompt: "Monitor X posts, comments and interactions for <mention our brand name, store locations and common misspellings>. <Include related hashtags and keywords associated with customer experience in retail>."
- **Analyse Sentiment Trends:**
Prompt: "Analyse the sentiment of X posts related to our brand <include brand details> over the past 24 hours. Identify any significant changes in sentiment and highlight potential causes."
- **Identify Emerging Issues:**
Prompt: "Review recent X posts about our brand <include brand details> and identify the top five most frequently mentioned customer pain points. Provide examples of representative posts for each issue."
- **Track Viral Content:**
Prompt: "Alert me to any X posts about our brand <include brand details> that have received over 1000 likes or 500 retweets in the last 6 hours. Summarize the content and sentiment of these posts."
- **Compare Online vs. Traditional Feedback:**
Prompt: "Compare the sentiment and issues raised in X posts about our brand <include brand details>

over the past week with our most recent NPS survey results. Identify any discrepancies or blind spots in our traditional feedback methods."
- **Generate Actionable Insights:**
Prompt: "Based on the X data analysed for our brand <include brand details>, provide three actionable recommendations to improve customer experience in our stores. Include potential impact and implementation difficulty for each."
- **Monitor Competitor Sentiment:**
Prompt: "Analyse X posts mentioning our top three competitors for our brand <include brand details>. Compare sentiment trends and identify any positive experiences we could potentially implement."
- **Create Executive Summary:**
Prompt: "Generate a daily executive summary of X sentiment analysis, including key metrics, emerging issues and recommended actions for our brand <include brand details>. Limit to one page with visualizations."

Best Practices for Framing Sentiment Analysis Prompts

1. Be specific about the timeframes and metrics you want to analyse (e.g. "past 24 hours", "posts with over 1000 likes").
2. Include instructions for categorizing and prioritizing information to avoid information overload.

3. Request actionable insights and recommendations, not just raw data or analysis.

How to Keep Your Data Safe

- **Disallow Grok from using your prompts and files for model training** by disabling data sharing in the Privacy and Safety settings of your X account. Uncheck the box labelled: "Allow your posts as well as your interactions, inputs and results with Grok to be used for training and fine-tuning".
- **Regularly clear your Grok conversation history** that contains sensitive customer sentiment analyses after extracting the required insights.
- **Schedule periodic reviews of your Grok usage and security settings** to ensure ongoing compliance with your company's data protection policies.

Smart Ways to Review AI Output

- **Compare Grok's X-based sentiment analysis** with data from your internal customer service logs and sales records to identify any disparities or blind spots.
- **Flag instances** where Grok's interpretation of customer sentiment seems inconsistent with established customer behavior patterns in your retail locations.

- Evaluate whether Grok's analysis properly accounts for **regional and seasonal factors** relevant to your retail business context.
- **Look for vague conclusions** about customer satisfaction trends and request more specific evidence from actual customer conversations.

Outcome

By leveraging Grok's real-time sentiment analysis, the retail chain closed the gap between structured feedback and organic customer conversations happening online. Instead of relying on delayed survey data, they could now detect emerging frustrations as they unfolded, track viral discussions and respond before issues spiralled into PR crises. This AI-driven approach enabled leadership to stay ahead of customer sentiment, turning reactive damage control into proactive experience management. What was once an unseen risk became a strategic advantage – ensuring customer trust wasn't just measured, but actively maintained in real time.

This chapter was written with the help of ChatGPT 4o Canvas and Perplexity.ai.

9

Strategic AI Literacy: THINKS

"Our mission is to solve intelligence—and then use it to solve everything else."

— DEMIS HASSABIS

Nalanda: Ancient India's Knowledge Ecosystem

In the ancient kingdom of Magadha, in what is now Bihar, India, stood Nalanda – a marvel of intellectual achievement that flourished for nearly 800 years, from the fifth to the twelfth century CE. More than just a university, Nalanda represented humanity's most ambitious early attempt to create a comprehensive knowledge ecosystem, drawing scholars from across Asia who sought to expand the boundaries of human thought.

At its height, Nalanda housed over 10,000 students and 2,000 teachers. Its vast libraries, the Dharmaganja or "Treasury of Truth", contained hundreds of thousands of volumes in a time when each manuscript represented years of painstaking work. What made Nalanda truly revolutionary, however, wasn't just its scale but its approach to knowledge integration and dialectical reasoning.

Three aspects of Nalanda's intellectual system particularly stand out as precursors to what we now seek in augmented cognition:

1. **Integrative Knowledge Architecture**: Unlike many institutions that separated disciplines, Nalanda's curriculum required students to master multiple knowledge domains – logic, mathematics, medicine, grammar, metaphysics, astronomy – creating scholars with unprecedented integrative thinking abilities. This cross-disciplinary approach enabled insights that specialized knowledge alone could not produce.
2. **Structured Dialectical Reasoning**: Dialectical reasoning is a method of thinking and discussion in which different ideas or viewpoints are examined and compared to reach a deeper understanding or truth. Nalanda pioneered a sophisticated science of debate, rigorously testing ideas through structured dialectical exchanges.
3. **Collaborative Intelligence Network**: Perhaps most remarkably, Nalanda functioned as a network of minds rather than a collection of individual thinkers. Scholar-monks practised formal debates where ideas were refined through collective intellectual engagement. Knowledge wasn't conceived as belonging to individuals but as emerging from a dynamic system of structured interactions.

The Chinese Buddhist monk, scholar, traveller and translator Xuanzang, who studied at Nalanda in the 7th century, described scholars who could explain the most profound doctrines and analyse the most complex ideas, making them accessible through powerful reasoning methods. The university's reputation was such that merely having studied there conferred intellectual authority across Asia.

Today, we stand at a similar inflection point in human history. Artificial intelligence, particularly in its advanced reasoning capacities, represents the most significant cognitive augmentation tool humanity has created since perhaps the systems of logic and dialectic that Nalanda's scholars formalized.

This potential is already being realized. A study involving a randomized controlled trial of 776 professionals at Procter and Gamble revealed fascinating insights about human–AI collaboration.[1]

- When strategically paired with systems like GPT-4, teams produced solutions ranked in the top 10 per cent of quality 2.3x more often than traditional groups, while individuals achieved results rivalling entire teams.
- AI erased expertise silos – novice analysts generated insights matching seasoned strategists, and engineers spontaneously integrated market dynamics into technical designs.

---

[1] Mollick, Ethan. 2025. "The Cybernetic Teammate." Oneusefulthing.org. One Useful Thing. March 22, 2025. https://www.oneusefulthing.org/p/the-cybernetic-teammate.

- Crucially, this cognitive partnership operated synergistically: teams saved 12–16 per cent time while producing 40 per cent more detailed outputs, and users experienced significantly higher levels of excitement, energy and enthusiasm alongside reduced anxiety.

Modern AI-augmented tools transform competition between human and machine intelligence into a new kind of co-evolution, where the strengths of both are amplified through collaboration.

The THINKS Framework: Integrating Strategic Cognition with AI

Just as Nalanda created methods to transcend the limitations of individual cognition, we now have the opportunity to leverage AI as an unprecedented thinking partner.

On that note, we introduce THINKS framework, which encapsulates this transformation by emphasizing how AI can be strategically integrated into thought processes. THINKS stands for:

- **Thought Leadership:** Leverage AI to identify emerging trends, analyse industry disruptions and position your organization as a thought leader in its domain. Anticipate future challenges and opportunities.

- **Human Resources and Human-Agent Optimization:** Optimize talent acquisition, employee development and performance management with AI. Enhance workforce productivity, engagement and retention through data-driven insights.

- **Innovation and Brainstorming:** Use AI to generate new ideas, explore diverse perspectives and accelerate the innovation process. Foster a culture of creativity and breakthrough thinking within your organization.

- **New Product Development:** Leverage AI throughout the product development life cycle, from ideation and design to testing and launch. Create innovative products that meet market needs and exceed customer expectations.

- **Knowledge Management – Using AI as a Second Brain:** Build a dynamic knowledge repository with AI. Capture, organize and retrieve critical information seamlessly, empowering your team with a collective "second brain" for enhanced decision-making.

- **Strategic Planning and Foresight:** Embed AI-driven forecasting into long-term planning to pre-empt risks and seize opportunities.

The THINKS framework is designed to help leaders and organizations harness AI as a cognitive partner, augmenting human thinking rather than replacing it. It focuses on leveraging AI to enhance critical thinking, reasoning, creativity and strategic planning.

Now, let's explore each component of the THINKS framework and its impact on strategic cognition and decision-making.

Thought Leadership

In boardrooms around the world, the most pressing question isn't just "What's happening now?" but also "What happens next?" Leaders who successfully navigate disruption aren't merely reacting to change – they're anticipating it, shaping the conversation and positioning their organizations at the forefront of industry evolution.

Yet traditional approaches to thought leadership are increasingly unable to keep pace. The volume of information has exploded, industry boundaries have blurred and the rate of technological change has accelerated beyond human capacity for anyone to be able to process it all. How can any organization hope to spot meaningful patterns in this noise, let alone translate them into strategic advantage?

This is where AI is fundamentally redefining what thought leadership means in the digital age. It's not just about having access to more information; it's also about having the computational power to identify hidden patterns, detect weak signals of change and connect seemingly unrelated trends into coherent strategic narratives. The most forward-thinking leaders aren't just using AI as a tool; they're partnering with it to expand their cognitive horizons and reimagine what's possible.

But what does this transformation look like in practice? How are organizations leveraging AI to anticipate market shifts, identify emerging opportunities and position themselves as visionaries in their respective fields? Let's explore this example.

From Data Dump to Visionary Narrative

We were working with the CEO of a mid-sized IT services firm preparing for a major industry conference in late 2024. He was scheduled to deliver the opening keynote. His team had provided him with a mountain of information – recent project successes, market analysis reports, internal capability assessments and analyst briefings. The CEO, a brilliant technologist, was drowning in the details. His initial draft attempts were data-heavy, technically accurate, but lacked a compelling narrative and a forward-looking vision that would resonate with a diverse audience of executives, potential clients and partners. He confessed during a coaching session, "I know what we do, but I'm struggling to articulate where the industry is going and why we matter in that future. I need to inspire, not just inform." The pain point was the gap between having the information and synthesizing it into a powerful, thought-leading message that established both him and his company as visionary.

AI Tool Recommendation

To accomplish this, we performed **tool chaining**, leveraging the strengths of both **Claude 3 Sonnet** and **ChatGPT Voice**. Tool chaining is a technique where the output of one AI tool or process is used as the input for another, creating a sequential workflow.

1. Claude 3 Sonnet

   Claude 3 Sonnet was selected as the primary tool for this scenario due to its advanced capabilities in understanding, synthesizing and generating high-quality narratives tailored to specific needs. Key reasons include:
   - **Narrative Generation and Synthesis:** Claude is good at transforming complex and diverse data (e.g. market analysis, project success stories) into a cohesive and compelling story arc, addressing the CEO's challenge of crafting a visionary narrative.
   - **Contextual Understanding:** Its ability to process large volumes of information (~200k context window) while maintaining coherence ensures that no critical detail is lost while simplifying the message for a diverse audience.
   - **Tone and Persona Adoption:** Claude can mimic specific leadership tones (e.g. visionary,

authoritative) and maintain consistency throughout the text, aligning with the CEO's need to inspire rather than just inform.

2. **ChatGPT Voice**

ChatGPT Voice complements Claude by offering dynamic conversational capabilities that enhance the refinement process. Reasons for its inclusion are:

- **Interactive Refinement:** ChatGPT Voice allows for iterative discussions, enabling the CEO to speak with AI and explore different angles, refine ideas and test how well the narrative resonates with diverse audiences.
- **Real-Time Feedback:** It provides immediate suggestions and adjustments, making it easier to fine-tune tone, clarity and engagement.
- **Audience Simulation:** ChatGPT can simulate responses from different audience personas (e.g. executives, clients), helping tailor the keynote to resonate effectively.

By combining these tools, the CEO gains both a sophisticated writing partner (Claude 3 Sonnet) and an interactive collaborator (ChatGPT Voice), enabling him to transform raw data into an inspiring keynote that positions him as a visionary leader.

Strategic AI Literacy: THINKS

Suggested Prompt (Claude)

- **Persona:** Act as an expert keynote speechwriter and strategic communications consultant, specializing in the IT services industry. Your client is the CEO of a mid-sized firm (Firm Name) focused on (e.g., Cloud Migration, Cybersecurity, Data Analytics services). The audience is C-level executives and technology leaders at the (Conference Name) conference. The desired tone is visionary, inspiring, confident, yet accessible.
- **Context:** The CEO needs to deliver a 20-minute opening keynote. We have source materials including: [List source material types, e.g. latest quarterly results summary, key client case study summaries (Company A - challenge/solution/outcome), internal R&D project overview on AI-driven automation, recent industry analyst report on cloud trends, competitor benchmark summary]. The core message should be about the next wave of digital transformation and (Firm Name)'s unique role in enabling it. Avoid overly technical jargon.

Task:
1. **Identify Core Theme:** Based on the provided context and source material types (imagine reviewing them), identify one central, forward-looking theme for the keynote (e.g. "The Rise of the Autonomous Enterprise", "Beyond Digital: The Cognitive Transformation", "Human-AI Collaboration as the New Competitive Edge"). Justify the choice briefly.

2. **Outline Keynote Structure:** Propose a five-section structure for the 20-minute keynote (e.g. Introduction/Hook, The Shifting Landscape, Our Vision/Approach, Proof Points/Case Study, Call to Action/Future Outlook).
3. **Draft Introduction (Hook):** Write a compelling opening (approx. 150–200 words) that grabs the audience's attention, introduces the core theme and establishes the CEO's credibility. Use the visionary tone.
4. **Develop "Vision" Section Content:** Draft the core content (approx. 300–400 words) for the "Our Vision/Approach" section. Synthesize insights from the potential source materials (R&D, analyst reports) to paint a picture of the future state and how (Firm Name)'s philosophy/services uniquely address it.
5. **Suggest Storytelling Elements:** Identify two to three opportunities within the structure to incorporate brief storytelling elements (e.g. referencing a specific client challenge from the case studies, an anecdote about the R&D journey).
6. **Propose Closing Statement:** Draft a powerful closing statement (approx. 100 words) that reinforces the core theme and leaves the audience with a clear call to action or a thought-provoking idea.

Output Format: Present the response clearly sectioned as per the tasks (theme, structure, introduction, vision content, storytelling elements, closing). Ensure the drafted sections adopt the specified visionary tone.

Suggested Prompt (ChatGPT Voice)

- **Persona:** Act as a professional keynote speech coach and feedback expert with a specialization in IT services industry conferences. Your role is to listen to my keynote speech delivery, provide constructive feedback on tone, clarity, engagement and audience resonance, and suggest improvements to make the speech visionary and inspiring.
- **Context:** I am practising the opening keynote for a major industry conference (Conference Name), where I aim to position myself and my company (Firm Name) as thought leaders in the next wave of digital transformation. The audience includes C-level executives, technology leaders, potential clients and partners. My speech is based on themes like (insert theme here, e.g. "Human-AI collaboration as the new competitive edge"), supported by insights from recent project successes, market analysis reports, internal R&D findings and industry trends.

Task:
1. Listen to my keynote speech as I deliver it in real time.
2. Once I ask you to, please provide actionable feedback on:
   - **Tone:** Does the speech sound visionary, inspiring, confident, yet accessible?
   - **Clarity:** Are the ideas presented clearly and easy to follow?

- **Engagement:** Does the narrative resonate with a diverse audience? Are there moments that feel too technical or dry?
- **Structure:** Is the speech well-organized with a compelling introduction, cohesive middle sections and a strong closing?

3. Suggest improvements to enhance storytelling elements (e.g. anecdotes or case studies) and refine the call to action.
4. Simulate audience responses from different personas (e.g. executives, clients) to test how well the speech resonates with each group.

Output Format: Provide feedback in a conversational manner after each section of my speech delivery. Include specific suggestions for improvement and simulate audience reactions where applicable.

Prompting Best Practices Followed

1. **Role and Tone Specification:** Both prompts clearly specify the role of the AI model and the desired tone to ensure the output aligns with the task's context. For Claude, the prompt defines it as an "expert keynote speechwriter and strategic communications consultant" with a "visionary, inspiring, confident, yet accessible" tone. For ChatGPT Voice, it positions the model as

a "professional keynote speech coach and feedback expert". This precise role definition guides the AI in producing contextually appropriate and purposeful outputs.
2. **Contextual Grounding with Detailed Instructions:** The prompts effectively anchor the AI's response by providing comprehensive context. For example, Claude's prompt includes details such as the CEO's firm size, industry focus, audience profile and the desired keynote theme. ChatGPT Voice's prompt similarly outlines the conference setting, audience type and the CEO's objective. By including contextual elements and specifying the desired structure (e.g. theme, structure, drafted intro), the prompts ensure that the output is both relevant and structured.
3. **Interactive and Real-Time Refinement:** The ChatGPT Voice prompt incorporates an interactive element by requesting real-time feedback and audience simulation. This dynamic approach allows the CEO to iteratively improve the keynote through conversational exchanges, testing the resonance of different narrative styles.

How to Use the Tool

1. Access Claude 3.7 Sonnet: https://claude.ai/.
2. Paste the prompt, customizing (Firm Name), (Conference Name), service focus and source material

types. You can optionally upload key source documents if the tool version supports it and privacy allows or rely on the prompt's description of them.
3. Execute the prompt.
4. Review the generated theme, structure and draft sections.
5. Iterate with follow-up prompts: "Refine the introduction to be more provocative", "Expand on the 'cognitive transformation' idea in the 'Vision' section using insights from the analyst report", "Rewrite the closing to be more actionable".
6. The CEO and team use the AI-generated structure and drafts as a strong starting point, refining it with their authentic voice and specific examples.
7. Use ChatGPT Voice via mobile app, leverage the suggested prompt and practise.

How to Keep Your Data Safe

- Instead of uploading full sensitive documents, provide summaries or **anonymized versions of case studies and internal data** within the prompt or supplementary text.
- After completing the task, **delete conversation histories** and temporary files to minimize data retention.
- **For Claude, be aware that conversations are not used for training by default**, except in specific cases like feedback or trust and safety reviews; avoid providing sensitive information in feedback.

- **For ChatGPT, opt out of allowing OpenAI to use your conversations for model training.** This can be done under the "Data Controls" section in settings.

Smart Ways to Review AI Output

- Does the generated language sound like the CEO? **Read sections aloud.** The AI provides a draft; the final delivery must be authentic. Edit heavily for voice.
- Does the proposed "vision" genuinely align with the company's strategic direction and capabilities, or is it generic industry hype? Ensure the message is ambitious but grounded. **Validate the vision** being articulated.
- **Check the logical flow** and transitions between the proposed sections. Does the story build effectively? Does the call to action logically follow the vision and proof points?
- Share key drafted passages (like the intro or vision statement) with a **trusted internal group.** Does it resonate? Is it inspiring? Does it clearly articulate the intended message?

Outcome

The Claude–ChatGPT Voice tool chaining approach transformed the CEO's presentation, combining Claude's narrative synthesis with ChatGPT's interactive feedback. This powerful pairing converted technical, discrete data into a visionary keynote that helped establish thought leadership and laid the groundwork for new business opportunities.

Human resources and Human-agent Optimization

The fundamental challenge of leadership has always been about talent – finding it, developing it and creating the conditions for exceptional performance. But today's organizations face unprecedented complexity in workforce management: remote and hybrid work arrangements, multi-generational workforces, skills shortages and the integration of AI into everyday workflows.

Traditional HR approaches – annual performance reviews, standardized training programs, and intuition-based hiring – are proving inadequate in this new landscape. They're too slow, too subjective, and too limited in their ability to personalize development at scale. Meanwhile, the cost of making the wrong people decisions continues to rise.

This is where AI is transforming human resources from an administrative function into a strategic advantage. By analysing vast amounts of workforce data, AI can reveal hidden patterns in employee engagement, predict flight risks before they manifest, identify skill gaps before they become critical and match talent to opportunities with unprecedented precision. More importantly, it's enabling a fundamental shift from human-only to human–agent teams, where AI handles routine tasks while humans focus on high-value creative and strategic work.

The question remains: how do innovative organizations bring these capabilities to life? The following example sheds light.

Hiring Bottleneck: A Recruitment Crisis

In March 2025, during an executive AI bootcamp, we sat across from the visibly exhausted Head of Talent Acquisition at a growing tech company.

"We're drowning in applications," they confessed, showing us their dashboard. "For our senior developer position, we received 547 résumé in two weeks. My team has spent over 80 hours on initial screening and we're barely halfway through."

Their hiring pipeline revealed dozens of open positions with hundreds of stalled candidates. "Last month, our VP of Engineering was furious because we lost two exceptional candidates while their applications sat in our review queue for three weeks. My recruiters are already working evenings and weekends."

The consequences were evident: delayed product launches, overworked staff and a hiring process that compromised diversity. "Unconscious bias creeps in when rushing through hundreds of applications," they admitted.

"With our current resources, we can't be both thorough and timely."

These pain points – excessive manual screening time, talent pipeline delays, compromised hiring quality and recruiter burnout – were threatening not just their talent acquisition strategy but the company's overall growth trajectory.

AI Tool Recommendation

To address the overwhelming volume of résumés and improve the hiring process, **Smallest.ai** is an excellent choice. This voice AI tool streamlines initial screening by conducting automated, unbiased interviews, quickly assessing candidate responses and filtering top talent based on predefined criteria. It stands out due to:

- **Lightning-Fast Response:** Smallest.ai's proprietary Lightning Text-to-Speech (TTS) model generates ultra-realistic audio at unmatched speeds.
- **Exceptional Voice Quality:** With a Mean Opinion Score (MOS) of 4.14, it surpasses competitors, ensuring high-quality synthetic speech.
- **Efficient Voice Cloning:** Smallest.ai can replicate human voices using only 5 seconds of audio input, significantly faster than competitors requiring 30

> seconds. This allows for personalized candidate engagement during screenings.
>
> By leveraging Smallest.ai, recruiters can reduce manual effort, accelerate hiring timelines and improve candidate experience.

How to Use Smallest.ai

1. **Set Up Smallest.ai:**
   - Visit https://atoms.smallest.ai/ and log in with your credentials.
   - Access the "Atoms" menu to begin creating a Voice AI agent.
2. **Create Your Agent:**
   - Click on "Create Agent" and select "Create from Scratch".
   - Configure the agent with:
     - Call Logs: Enable to track interactions.
     - Assistant Name: Assign a relevant name (e.g. "RecruiterBot").
     - Description: Briefly describe its purpose (e.g. "Screening candidates for senior developer positions").
     - Phone Number: Set for inbound/outbound calls.

3. **Configure Key Settings:**
   - **LLM Configuration:** Choose the desired AI model and set the language to English (enable multilingual support if needed).
   - **Synthesizer Configuration:** Set speed to medium and select a voice option like "Chetan" or "Lightning".
   - **Knowledge Base:** Link a global knowledge base for decision-making.
4. **Design the Workflow:**
   - Create logical nodes for automated interviews:
     - Node 1: Greeting and interest confirmation.
     - Node 2: Collect candidate details (e.g. experience, location).
     - Node 3: Provide company information.
     - Node 4: Schedule follow-ups if necessary.
     - Node 5: Handle disinterest and gather feedback.
     - Node 6: Thank the candidate and end the call.
   - Connect these nodes seamlessly to automate the screening process.
5. **Launch and Monitor:**
   - Deploy the agent and monitor call logs to ensure smooth operations.

How to Keep Your Data Safe

- Smallest.ai operates using small language models hosted within the organization's premises. This ensures

that **sensitive candidate data remains under the organization's control**, minimizing risks associated with cloud-based storage and external data transfers.
- **All communication between user devices and Smallest.ai is encrypted** using secure HTTPS connections. This prevents unauthorized interception of sensitive information during transmission.
- **Sensitive candidate information should be anonymized** wherever possible, reducing exposure to privacy risks while maintaining usability for recruitment purposes.

Smart Ways to Review AI Output

- **Compare the AI's candidate rankings with human evaluations** to ensure they meet the job requirements accurately.
- **Conduct spot checks on recorded interviews** to identify any inaccuracies or biases in the AI's assessments.
- **Gather input from your recruitment team** on whether the tool's output aligns with their expectations and improves efficiency.
- Ensure that the AI's **screening criteria align with the specific needs of the position** and the company's hiring standards.
- **Review AI-generated reports** or summaries for any vague assessments and seek clarification or additional information as needed.

Outcome

Smallest.ai's voice AI presented a fresh lens for the talent acquisition team to approach their overwhelming application bottleneck. In its early implementation stages, the team began reaping benefits through automated screenings, showing promise for reducing recruiter burnout while maintaining hiring quality.

Innovation and Brainstorming

The innovation paradox has never been more acute: organizations face mounting pressure to innovate faster and more radically, yet human creativity remains constrained by our cognitive limitations. We struggle to think beyond our expertise, succumb to groupthink and unknowingly recycle ideas rather than generating truly novel concepts.

Traditional approaches to innovation – brainstorming sessions, suggestion boxes, stage-gate processes – were designed for an era of relative stability and homogeneous thinking. They work well for incremental improvements but often fail to produce the breakthrough ideas organizations need to thrive amid disruption. The result? Innovation portfolios heavy on safe bets but light on gamechangers.

AI is now rewriting the rules of creativity and innovation. Rather than simply automating existing processes, it's expanding the boundaries of what's possible by exploring solution spaces too vast for human minds to comprehend, connecting disparate fields of knowledge and generating thousands of options that humans can then evaluate and refine. Rather than replace human creativity, this amplifies it and removes the constraints that have limited our innovative potential.

But what does this AI-enhanced innovation process look like in practice? How are leading organizations leveraging these capabilities to accelerate ideation, diversify their thinking and breakthrough long-standing constraints? Let's examine this example that illustrates these principles in action.

Diversifying Perspectives in Senior Care Service Design

During an AI bootcamp with a leading senior-care provider, the team was brainstorming new services to enhance resident well-being and family connectivity. While deeply experienced, the team realized their perspectives were somewhat limited, often defaulting to solutions based on their existing operational models or most vocal resident feedback. The Head of Innovation remarked, "We think we know what our residents and their families need, but are we truly considering the diversity of experiences? The quiet resident, the tech-savvy caregiver daughter, the son living abroad, the resident with early cognitive decline – are we designing for them?" The pain point was a potential empathy gap and a lack of diverse user perspectives hindering truly resident-centric innovation. They needed a way to step outside their own assumptions.

> ## AI Tool Recommendation
>
> **Gemini 2.5** is a thinking model, designed to tackle increasingly complex problems. Here are the aligned capabilities of Gemini 2.5 Pro that make it a good fit for this task:
>
> - **Enhanced Reasoning for Persona Creation:** Gemini 2.5 Pro excels at reasoning through complex prompts, enabling it to generate nuanced, diverse and empathetic user personas. Its ability to incorporate context and draw logical conclusions ensures that the personas reflect realistic motivations, frustrations and needs relevant to the senior care sector. The model's reasoning capabilities allow it to simulate a variety of perspectives (e.g. residents with different health statuses or tech-savvy family members), ensuring diversity across personas.
> - **Empathy and Context Awareness:** By integrating context-aware reasoning directly into its base model, Gemini 2.5 Pro can create rich narratives that evoke empathy. This is particularly valuable for crafting "day in the life" snippets and understanding user

frustrations and goals. It can effectively capture subtle nuances, such as the emotional challenges faced by family members living abroad or residents with cognitive impairments.
- **Efficiency in Iterative Refinement:** Gemini 2.5 Pro can quickly refine outputs based on feedback or additional prompts, making it ideal for iterative persona development during workshops or brainstorming sessions.

Suggested Prompt

- **Persona:** Act as an expert ethnographer and service designer specializing in the senior care sector. You excel at creating rich, empathetic user personas to inform innovation.
- **Context:** A senior care provider [Provider Name] wants to brainstorm new services to enhance resident well-being and family connectivity. The innovation team needs diverse perspectives beyond their typical assumptions. Key areas for innovation include: [List two to three areas, e.g. reducing social isolation, improving family communication/updates, facilitating intergenerational activities, supporting residents with mild cognitive impairment].

Task:
- Generate **four distinct and detailed user personas** relevant to the senior care context. Ensure diversity across factors like resident health/mobility, cognitive status, tech-savviness, family involvement level and socioeconomic background. For each persona, include:
- **Name and Photo Description:** A fictional name and a brief description suitable for generating a representative image later (e.g. "Shalini, 82, warm smile, enjoys knitting, slightly frail but bright eyes").
- **Background & Situation:** Brief story covering their life before moving to care (if resident) or their relationship/situation (if family member), current health/mobility/cognitive status (if resident), living situation (if family).
- **Technology Usage:** Describe their comfort level and usage habits with technology (e.g. "Uses a simple smartphone for calls/texts, enjoys emailed photos," or "Tech-savvy, uses video calls, online portals, wearables").
- **Goals and Needs (related to care/connectivity):** What are they trying to achieve or what do they need the most? (e.g. Resident: "Maintain independence", "Stay connected with grandkids overseas". Family: "Peace of mind about daily well-being", "Easier way to coordinate visits").
- **Frustrations and Pain Points (related to care/connectivity):** What challenges or difficulties do they

face? (e.g. Resident: "Feeling lonely in the evenings", "Difficulty using the complex TV remote". Family: "Getting timely updates after a health incident", "Feeling guilty for not visiting more often").
- **A "Day in the Life" Snippet:** A short paragraph illustrating a typical interaction or challenge related to the innovation areas (e.g. "Sujata struggling to join a group video call"; "Her son abroad checking a confusing portal for updates").

Output Format: Structure each persona clearly with the six specified headings. Ensure the personas are distinct and offer unique perspectives relevant to the innovation areas.

Prompting Best Practices Followed

1. **Persona Diversity Instruction:** Explicitly requesting diversity across specific factors (health, tech-savviness, family role) guides the AI to create varied profiles.
2. **Rich Detail Specification:** Asking for specific categories like goals, frustrations, and a "day in the life" snippet prompts the AI to generate deeper, more empathetic personas than simple demographic lists.
3. **Contextual Grounding:** Linking the persona generation task to specific innovation areas (social isolation, family communication) ensures the personas are relevant to the brainstorming purpose.

How to Use the Tool

1. Access Gemini 2.5 via https://gemini.google.com/.
2. Customize the prompt with the provider's name and specific innovation focus areas.
3. Execute the prompt to generate the initial set of personas.
4. The innovation team uses these AI-generated personas during brainstorming sessions. They can "role-play" as the persona or ask "How would Sujata feel about this idea?"
5. Use follow-up prompts to flesh out personas or create new ones: "Create a persona for a caregiver spouse visiting daily", or "Expand on the frustrations of the tech-savvy daughter persona."
6. *(Optional)* Use the photo descriptions with an image generation tool (like Midjourney or DALL.E) to create visual representations of the personas for the workshop.

How to Keep Your Data Safe

- Gemini 2.5 Pro **employs state-of-the-art encryption techniques** to protect data during transmission (in transit) and storage (at rest). This ensures that sensitive information, such as resident or family details, is safeguarded from unauthorized access.

- Disable the "Activity in Gemini Applications" setting if you do not want conversations stored for extended periods.[2] When this setting is off, interactions are retained for a maximum of 72 hours solely for service delivery purposes, reducing long-term data exposure.

Smart Ways to Review AI Output

- **Perform Authenticity and Believability Check:** Do the personas feel like plausible representations of individuals in the senior-care ecosystem, or are they caricatures? Do their goals and frustrations seem realistic? Refine details for authenticity.
- **Perform Diversity Coverage Audit:** Did the AI generate sufficient diversity across the requested factors (age, tech use, health, family role)? Are there any critical perspectives still missing (e.g. low-income background, non-English speaking)? Generate additional personas if needed.
- **Avoid Stereotyping:** While creating distinct profiles, check that the AI hasn't relied on harmful stereotypes related to age, health conditions or technology use. Ensure the personas are respectful and nuanced.

---

[2] "Gemini Apps Privacy Hub - Gemini Apps Help." 2019. Google.com. https://tinyurl.com/3jsdcytk.

Outcome

By integrating Gemini 2.5 Pro into their innovation process, the senior-care provider could generate diverse, empathetic user personas that reflect the unique needs of residents and their families. This approach bridges the empathy gap, enabling the design of truly resident-centric services that address challenges like social isolation, intergenerational engagement and cognitive support.

New Product Development

The stakes in product development have never been higher. Market windows are shrinking, competition is intensifying, and customer expectations are constantly rising. Yet the process remains fraught with uncertainty: Will customers actually want this product? Will it solve their problems effectively? Can we build it on time and on budget?

Traditional approaches to product development – lengthy requirements gathering, sequential design processes, limited prototyping – simply can't keep pace with today's market realities. They're too slow, too expensive and too disconnected from evolving customer needs. The result is a sobering statistic: the majority of new products still fail, representing billions in wasted resources and missed opportunities.

AI is now transforming every phase of the product development life cycle – from initial ideation to design, testing and launch. It's enabling organizations to rapidly explore thousands of design alternatives, predict customer preferences with remarkable accuracy, simulate product performance under countless scenarios and optimize manufacturing processes before the first unit is produced. This isn't just accelerating the process; it's fundamentally improving the quality of decisions throughout the development journey.

But how are leading organizations implementing these capabilities in ways that complement rather than replace human expertise? What lessons can we learn from their successes and challenges? Let's explore this illuminating case study that demonstrates these principles in action.

Product Integration Bottleneck: A Cross-Team Collaboration Crisis

In February 2025, during a strategic offsite, we sat across from the visibly frustrated Chief Product Officer at a major telecommunication provider.

"We're falling behind our competitors," they confessed, showing me their market analysis dashboard. "Our rivals have already launched integrated communication apps while our features remain scattered across disconnected products. We're losing market share every week we delay."

Their product roadmap revealed siloed development across messaging, voice and cloud collaboration divisions. "Last quarter, I discovered that three separate teams were building nearly identical AI scheduling assistants. We're wasting millions on duplicated efforts, and sharing the prototype across teams was a pain."

The consequences were evident: a disjointed user experience, inefficient resource allocation and delayed time-to-market. "Our users have to juggle multiple apps when competitors offer everything in one seamless experience," they admitted. "With our current structure, we can't be both innovative and cohesive."

These pain points – siloed development, duplicated efforts, fragmented user experience and prototype sharing difficulties – were threatening not just their product strategy but the company's overall market position in the rapidly evolving telecommunications landscape.

AI Tool Recommendation

In such situations, we recommend **Claude 3.7 Sonnet** as the smartest choice:

- **Context-Aware Strategic Planning:** Claude 3.7 Sonnet demonstrates exceptional ability to synthesize information from multiple sources – exactly what's needed when combining backlogs from three separate divisions and customer feedback. It can identify patterns, overlaps and integration opportunities across different divisions, helping to create a cohesive product strategy rather than just combining disparate features.

- **Superior Code Generation Capabilities**: Claude 3.7 Sonnet excels at generating clean, functional code across multiple languages. This is relevant for integrated communication app development, as it can help prototype shared components, create API integration layers between siloed systems and develop consistent UI elements that work across messaging, collaboration and conferencing features.
- **Collaborative Artifacts for Cross-Team Sharing**: Claude's sharable artifacts feature directly addresses your pain point of difficult prototype sharing. Teams can collaboratively develop and iterate on product specifications, roadmaps and technical documentation within the conversation. These artifacts can be easily shared across divisions, ensuring everyone works from the same foundation and eliminating the duplication issues that have plagued previous efforts.

Suggested Prompt

Act as a cross-functional product strategist for our telecom company that's developing an all-in-one communication app to compete with recent market entrants.

You have access to:
- Division A's messaging platform backlog (features include: end-to-end encryption, media sharing and group messaging capabilities)
- Division B's cloud-collaboration backlog (features include: document sharing, collaborative editing and project management tools)
- Division C's voice/video conferencing user stories (features include: HD video, screen sharing and AI-driven transcription)
- Consolidated feedback from our top 50 enterprise customers highlighting integration pain points and desired unified experience

Tasks:
- Write a compelling internal press release in Jeff Bezos's "working backwards" style that highlights our vision for this unified communication platform
- Develop a 12-month unified product roadmap with clear integration milestones
- Identify five to seven signature features that would differentiate our offering from competitors

- Propose a cross-functional team structure to break down existing silos
- Create a design system framework to ensure consistent UI/UX across all functionalities
- Outline potential technical integration challenges and proposed solutions
- Address regulatory considerations (data privacy, 5G integration, international compliance)

Follow-up Prompt for Prototype Development:

- Now help us create an interactive prototype of our unified communication app that can be shared across teams. Please:
  - Design key user flows for the three most important cross-functional features.
  - Generate interactive wireframes showing the unified interface across messaging, collaboration and conferencing.
  - Create a component library that ensures visual consistency.
  - Suggest a collaboration workflow that allows all three divisions to contribute to and test the prototype.
  - Recommend the most suitable prototyping tools that support real-time cross-team collaboration.
  - Outline a user testing approach to validate the integrated experience with our enterprise customers.

Prompting Best Practices Followed

1. **Specific Context and Resource Details**: Provided clear context about each division's capabilities and existing backlogs, allowing Claude to understand the full scope of the integration challenge.
2. **Clear Task Structure with Measurable Outputs**: Requested specific deliverables (12-month roadmap, five to seven signature features) rather than vague guidance, ensuring actionable results.
3. **Strategic Follow-up Prompting**: Created a dedicated follow-up prompt for the interactive prototype development, addressing the specific pain point of cross-team sharing while using precise language like "interactive wireframes" and "real-time cross-team collaboration".

How to Use the Tool

1. **Log on to Claude 3.7 Sonnet**: Visit https://claude.ai/ and sign in with your company credentials.
2. **Create a New Conversation**: Click "New Chat" and paste your initial strategic prompt with all the division backlog details.
3. **Save Key Artifacts**: When Claude generates the product roadmap and strategy documents, click the download button on any artifacts to save them locally.

Strategic AI Literacy: THINKS

4. **Submit the Follow-up Prompt:** Once the strategy is finalized, paste the interactive prototype follow-up prompt in the same conversation to maintain context.
5. **Share Results with Teams:** Download the completed prototype artifacts and distribute them to all three divisions through your company's secure file-sharing system.

How to Keep Your Data Safe

- **Rely on Claude's built-in security features,** which include not storing conversations long-term and robust data-handling protocols.
- When inputting customer feedback or other sensitive data, **remove identifying information** to protect privacy while retaining necessary insights.
- **Leveraged permissioned artifacts.** "Permissioned Artifacts" in Claude refer to using access controls within Claude's team plan to restrict who can view or edit specific artifacts containing sensitive information like product plans.

Smart Ways to Review AI Output

1. **Conduct Cross-Functional Review Sessions:** Have representatives from each division review Claude's output together to ensure all perspectives are considered.

2. **Perform Technical Feasibility Check:** Have engineering leads verify that the integrated features and prototype designs are technically viable within your current architecture.
3. **Ensure Customer Validation Alignment:** Compare Claude's proposed solutions against actual customer feedback to ensure the strategy addresses real user pain points.

Outcome

By leveraging Claude 3.7 Sonnet and the structured prompting approach, the telecommunications company successfully broke down their siloed development process. The interactive prototype became a unified focal point that all three divisions could contribute to and refine collaboratively.

Knowledge Management: Using AI as a Second Brain

In today's knowledge economy, an organization's most valuable asset isn't its physical capital, but the collective wisdom, expertise and insights of its people. Yet this critical resource remains largely trapped in silos – scattered across emails, documents, conversations and, most importantly, in the minds of individuals who may leave at any time.

Strategic AI Literacy: THINKS

Traditional knowledge management approaches — documents repositories, wikis, communities of practice — have struggled to overcome fundamental human limitations: we can't document everything we know, we don't have time to read everything others have documented, and we can't easily find the specific insights we need when we need them. The result is a persistent and costly pattern of reinventing wheels, repeating mistakes and failing to leverage existing expertise.

AI is now enabling a profound shift in how organizations capture, organize and activate their collective intelligence. By functioning as a "second brain" that can process, connect and retrieve information at superhuman scale, AI systems are breaking down knowledge silos, surfacing forgotten insights and making the right knowledge available to the right people at the right time. This isn't just making existing processes more efficient — it's creating entirely new capabilities for organizational learning and memory.

But what does this transformation look like in practice? How are forward-thinking organizations implementing these systems in ways that complement human cognition rather than replacing it? Let's examine this instructive example that demonstrates the potential of AI as a second brain.

Knowledge-rich but Insight-poor

During a review at a management consulting firm in March 2025, a senior partner highlighted a recurring inefficiency. "We conduct dozens of client projects and internal research studies every year, generating valuable insights. But that knowledge often stays siloed within project teams or buried in lengthy PDF reports on the server." When starting a new project, teams spent days searching for relevant past work, often redundantly researching topics already covered. Junior consultants struggled to quickly get up to speed on industry best practices documented internally.

With information scattered across different platforms and formats, the firm was experiencing a classic "garbage in, garbage out" problem – even when valuable insights existed, they couldn't be effectively synthesized or applied to new contexts. Additionally, this fragmentation meant teams were unable to leverage the strengths of modern AI tools, which require structured, accessible data to deliver meaningful intelligence.

The pain point: valuable institutional knowledge was fragmented and inaccessible, hindering efficiency, quality and the ability to build upon previous work effectively. They had a knowledge *repository*, but not a collective *brain*.

AI Tools Recommendation

Google NotebookLM is an excellent choice for such a scenario for the following reasons:

1. **Large Context Window:** NotebookLM leverages Google's latest Gemini model, which features an industry-leading context window of up to 2 million tokens. This allows the tool to process extensive amounts of information, such as thousands of pages of text or lengthy transcripts, simultaneously. For instance, with a context window of 2 million tokens, NotebookLM can handle up to 133 such 50-page PDFs in one notebook at the same time.
2. **Multimodal Source Flexibility:** NotebookLM supports diverse input formats, including PDFs, Google Docs, audio files and YouTube video transcripts. This versatility is ideal for consolidating knowledge scattered across different platforms and formats into one centralized repository.
3. **Source Grounding for Accuracy:** Source grounding in AI means connecting the model's outputs to specific, verifiable data sources, ensuring the information it generates is accurate, reliable and traceable to its original documents. NotebookLM provides traceable citations for its outputs by directly referencing the uploaded documents. This ensures

> that all insights and answers are rooted in reliable, internal knowledge rather than generic or unverified information, which is crucial for consulting teams working on high-stakes projects.

How to Set Up NotebookLM as a Second Brain

Follow these steps to set up NotebookLM in the context of the consulting firm:

1. **Create a New Notebook:** Start by navigating to Google NotebookLM and signing in with your Google account. Click on "Create" to set up a new notebook. Name it according to your project or topic (e.g. "Digital Transformation Strategies").
2. **Gather and Upload Documents**: Upload high-quality, relevant documents, reports and research materials related to your project. You can upload various formats like PDFs, Google Docs or even links to online resources. Avoid uploading outdated or irrelevant data – remember the principle of "garbage in, garbage out". In other words, the quality of insights depends on the quality of the input.
3. **Test Queries**: Use simple prompts to test the system's ability to retrieve accurate insights from your data (e.g. "What are the recurring challenges for retail banks in digital transformation?").

Strategic AI Literacy: THINKS

4. **Maintain and Update Regularly:** Periodically review and update your notebook to ensure it remains accurate and relevant. Remove outdated documents, add new findings or reports, and refine the content as needed. This step ensures that your "second brain" evolves with your projects and continues to deliver meaningful insights over time.

Suggested Prompt

Context: I am starting a new consulting project focused on digital transformation strategies for a mid-sized retail bank. I need to quickly leverage our firm's existing knowledge from past projects and research in this area.

Questions for the Knowledge Base

1. **Summarize Key Challenges:** Based only on the uploaded documents, what are the top three recurring challenges our firm has identified for mid-sized retail banks undergoing digital transformation? Cite the source documents for each challenge.
2. **Identify Success Factors:** What are the critical success factors for implementing digital transformation in retail banking, as highlighted in the case studies (mention specific case study names/identifiers if known, e.g. "Project Phoenix Debrief", "Bank Y Case Study")?

3. **Compare Approaches:** Did "Project Phoenix Debrief" and "Bank Y Case Study" propose different approaches regarding legacy system modernization? Summarize the key differences.
4. **Extract Best Practices:** Extract a list of actionable best practices mentioned across all documents related to customer onboarding in a digital banking environment.
5. **Find Contradictions:** Are there any conflicting findings or recommendations regarding the adoption of AI chatbots for customer service mentioned in the uploaded reports?

Prompting Best Practices Followed

1. **Be Specific and Contextual:** The prompt provides clear context ("digital transformation strategies for a mid-sized retail bank") and specifies what insights are needed (e.g. challenges, success factors). This ensures precise responses from NotebookLM.
2. **Structure Questions Clearly:** Each question is distinct, focused and actionable (e.g. "Compare Approaches" or "Find Contradictions"), which helps NotebookLM deliver targeted outputs without ambiguity.
3. **Reference Uploaded Content:** The prompt explicitly directs NotebookLM to base its answers only on uploaded documents, ensuring that responses are rooted in verified internal knowledge rather than generic information.

Strategic AI Literacy: THINKS

How to Use the Tool

1. **Upload Relevant Data**: Consolidate all internal reports, case studies and research into NotebookLM for centralized access.
2. **Ask Targeted Questions**: Use structured prompts like those provided above to extract specific insights from your knowledge base (e.g. identifying recurring challenges or comparing approaches).
3. **Synthesize Insights**: Review AI-generated summaries or comparisons to identify patterns, contradictions or actionable recommendations relevant to your project goals.
4. **Collaborate with Teams**: Share insights generated by NotebookLM with team members during project planning sessions to ensure alignment and informed decision-making.

How to Keep Your Data Safe

- Always **access NotebookLM on secure, private networks** (like your home or office Wi-Fi) to reduce the risk of unauthorized access.
- Only **share notebooks with people who need access**. Use the "viewer" role for those who just need to see the content but shouldn't edit it.
- If you're using NotebookLM on a shared device, make sure to **log out after your session to protect your data**.

Smart Ways to Review AI Output

- Cross-check AI-generated summaries or insights with original reports to ensure accuracy and avoid misinterpretation of critical information. **Always verify against source documents.**
- If something seems unclear or incomplete, ask NotebookLM a follow-up question to get more details or clarification. **Ask follow-up questions.**
- For critical topics, **cross-check AI-generated information with trusted external sources** or industry standards to confirm accuracy and reliability.

Outcome

By adopting Google NotebookLM as a centralized knowledge management tool, the consulting firm could transform its fragmented knowledge repository into an accessible "collective brain". Teams saved significant time during project initiation by quickly retrieving relevant insights from past work, reducing redundancy in research efforts while improving efficiency and quality of deliverables.

Strategic Planning and Foresight

The fundamental challenge of strategic planning remains unchanged: how to make sound decisions today that will position your organization for success in an uncertain tomorrow. Yet traditional approaches to planning and forecasting are increasingly inadequate in a world characterized by exponential change, complex interdependencies and black swan events.

Annual planning cycles, linear forecasting models and consensus-based decision-making were designed for more stable environments. They struggle to account for emergent threats, non-linear shifts and the complex interplay of technological, social, economic and environmental factors that shape our future. As a result, organizations are repeatedly blindsided by developments that, in retrospect, contained clear warning signals.

AI is now redefining what's possible in strategic foresight and planning. By processing vast amounts of structured and unstructured data, identifying weak signals of change, modelling complex scenarios, and continuously updating predictions as new information emerges, AI-augmented planning tools are helping leaders navigate uncertainty with greater confidence. This isn't about predicting the future with certainty – it's also about expanding our capacity to imagine possible futures and prepare for them systematically.

But how are leading organizations implementing these capabilities in ways that complement rather than replace human judgment? What lessons can we learn from their successes and challenges? Let's explore this case study that demonstrates these principles in action.

Analysis Paralysis, Decision Stalemate

During an executive retreat at a major leisure-and-hospitality company, the leadership team found themselves deadlocked while evaluating three strategic growth options that emerged from their annual planning process. Despite extensive market research, competitor analysis and internal performance data, the decision-making process had ground to a halt. "We've collected mountains of information and everyone has their own interpretation of what it means," noted the Chief Strategy Officer, "but we can't seem to reach consensus on which path to take."

The boardroom had become divided, with passionate advocates for each strategic option presenting compelling but conflicting analyses of the same data. One faction championed expanding their luxury portfolio, another pushed for investing in technology-enhanced experiences, while a third group advocated developing new mid-market brands.

Each department viewed the decision through their own lens: Finance focused on capital requirements and ROI projections, Marketing emphasized brand positioning and customer acquisition costs, while Operations worried about implementation challenges and staffing implications. "We're drowning in opinions and perspectives," sighed the CEO during a tense moment, "but we're no closer to a decision than when we started this retreat."

The pain point: despite having three well-researched strategic options, the company remained paralyzed by competing interpretations, departmental biases and an inability to synthesize diverse viewpoints into a unified direction, causing them to lose valuable market positioning time while competitors moved forward decisively.

> **AI Tool Recommendation**
>
> It's ChatGPT o3 to the rescue! Here's why:
> - **Problem Decomposition:** ChatGPT o3 excels at breaking down complex strategic decisions, identifying hidden patterns across conflicting perspectives and producing balanced evaluations – perfect for resolving the company's decision paralysis among competing options.
> - **Natural Language Understanding:** Its advanced natural language processing capabilities enable it to objectively synthesize contradictory viewpoints and data interpretations, helping teams overcome the departmental biases and personal attachments to specific strategies that are currently blocking consensus.
> - **Multi-scenario Analyser:** The model can efficiently evaluate multiple scenarios simultaneously, comparing the luxury portfolio expansion, technology-enhanced

> experiences and mid-market brand development options against consistent criteria while identifying potential hybrid approaches that might satisfy diverse stakeholder concerns.

Meta Prompt to Choose the Right Strategy Option

A meta prompt is a structured, high-level framework that guides how you interact with AI models to solve complex problems systematically. It organizes your thinking process and ensures comprehensive analysis. Here are the steps for resolving the strategic decision stalemate:

1. **Define Role and State Problem:** Begin by telling ChatGPT o3 to act as a strategic hospitality consultant and clearly state the decision paralysis between three strategic growth options.
2. **Brainstorm Solutions:** Instruct the model to evaluate each of the three existing options considering the perspectives of Finance, Marketing and Operations departments.
3. **Probability Evaluation:** Ask the model to evaluate the probability of success for each strategic option, assigning a percentage score from 1 per cent to 100 per cent, justifying these scores with pros, cons, implementation difficulties, market timing and competitive positioning.

4. **Isolate the Winner:** Have the model identify the strategy with the highest probability of success based on balanced criteria.
5. **Brainstorm Competitive Solutions:** Ask the model to create two hybrid or alternative approaches that combine strengths from multiple options.
6. **Probability Evaluation (Iteration 2):** Evaluate the probability of success for these new hybrid solutions.
7. **Isolate the Winner (Iteration 2):** Compare all options to determine the optimal strategic direction.
8. **Loop Steps 5–7 Three Times:** Continue refining hybrid solutions until reaching an optimal approach.

This meta prompt works by systematically moving from evaluation of existing options to creative generation of hybrid solutions through multiple iterations. It breaks through decision paralysis by providing progressively refined alternatives that incorporate the best elements of departmental perspectives while eliminating weaknesses, ultimately converging on an optimal strategy that balances diverse organizational priorities.

Suggested Prompt

You are an expert strategic consultant specializing in the leisure-and-hospitality industry. Our leadership team is experiencing decision paralysis while evaluating three

strategic growth options that emerged from our annual planning process:
1. **Strategy 1:** Include strategy details, including any relevant documents, market research, financial projections and implementation timelines.
2. **Strategy 2:** Include strategy details, including any relevant documents, market research, financial projections and implementation timelines.
3. **Strategy 3:** Include strategy details, including any relevant documents, market research, financial projections and implementation timelines.

- Each department views these options differently: Finance focuses on ROI and capital requirements, Marketing on brand positioning and customer acquisition, while Operations considers implementation and staffing challenges.
- Please evaluate these five options:
    - For each, explain why it might be viable and list three components that contribute to its potential success.
    - Then assign a probability of success percentage (1–100 per cent), justifying your score by analysing pros, cons, implementation difficulty, competitive landscape and expected outcomes.
    - After identifying the strongest option, propose two hybrid approaches that combine elements from multiple strategies.
    - Evaluate these new approaches using the same criteria.

- Continue this process of refinement twice more until you've identified the most balanced strategy that addresses our diverse departmental concerns while maximizing market opportunity.

Prompting Best Practices Followed

- **Clear Context Setting:** The prompt provides comprehensive background on the company's situation, the three competing strategies and departmental perspectives to ensure relevant analysis.
- **Structured Analytical Framework:** The prompt establishes a consistent evaluation methodology (pros/cons, implementation difficulty, expected outcomes) to enable objective comparison.
- **Iterative Refinement:** The prompt encourages progressive improvement through multiple rounds of hybrid solution development rather than settling for initial options.

How to Use the Tool

1. Go to ChatGPT.com
2. **Select ChatGPT o3 model** from the dropdown menu in the top-right corner of the interface.
3. **Copy and paste the suggested prompt** into the chat input field, replacing the strategy placeholders with your actual strategic options.

4. **Attach any relevant documents** using the paperclip icon to provide the AI with complete context about each strategy option.
5. **Review the initial analysis** of each strategy, noting especially the reasoning behind the probability scores rather than just the percentages themselves.
6. **Save the hybrid approaches** the model generates and share them with your leadership team to facilitate breaking through the decision paralysis.

How to Keep Your Data Safe

1. **Avoid sharing proprietary financial projections or competitive intelligence.** Focus on general strategic directions and considerations rather than sensitive figures.
2. **Clear conversation history** after strategic planning is complete.
3. **Review all AI outputs for accidental inclusion of confidential information** before sharing with the broader team.

Smart Ways to Review AI Output

1. **Cross-reference recommendations against existing market research** to validate the AI's strategic conclusions in real-world industry contexts.

2. **Have representatives from each department independently review** the analysis to ensure their perspectives are adequately represented.
3. **Conduct a sensitivity analysis** by slightly modifying assumptions to see if the recommended strategy remains robust under varied conditions.

Outcome

By blending seasoned leadership intuition with ChatGPT o3's objective analysis, the leisure-and-hospitality company overcame their decision stalemate. The leadership team embraced a phased hybrid approach that balanced immediate returns with long-term growth. This human–AI collaboration created confident consensus, accelerating implementation while competitors remained paralyzed by similar strategic dilemmas.

This chapter was written with the help of ChatGPT 4o Canvas and Perplexity.ai.

10

Agentic AI Literacy: DOES

"Ideas are easy. Execution is everything."
— JOHN DOERR

ISRO's Mangalyaan: When Execution Excellence Redefines Possibilities

On a clear November morning in 2013, the Polar Satellite Launch Vehicle (PSLV) C25 thundered skyward from the Satish Dhawan Space Centre in Sriharikota, carrying with it India's first interplanetary mission – Mangalyaan, the Mars Orbiter.[1] What followed was not just a remarkable achievement in space exploration but a masterclass in execution intelligence, resource optimization and operational excellence.

The world watched with scepticism. Mars missions had defeated space agencies with far more experience and

---

[1] Mehta, Jatan. 2021. "Mangalyaan, India's First Mars Mission." Edited by Planetary Society staff. The Planetary Society. https://tinyurl.com/e88kyuc9.

resources – indeed, more than half of all Mars missions had failed. Yet, just 10 months later, on 24 September 2014, Mangalyaan successfully entered Mars' orbit on its very first attempt, making ISRO the fourth space agency to reach Mars and the first to succeed on its maiden voyage.[2]

What made this achievement extraordinary wasn't merely reaching Mars – it was how ISRO accomplished this feat. Operating with a budget of approximately $74 million – less than the production cost of the Hollywood space movie *Gravity*[3] and roughly one-ninth the cost of NASA's contemporary MAVEN Mars mission – ISRO demonstrated three principles that embody the essence of effective execution:

1. **Strategic Autonomy and Decision Execution:** ISRO engineers designed Mangalyaan with unprecedented autonomy. The spacecraft could independently execute complex manoeuvres, manage power systems during the Mars orbit insertion and make critical adjustments without constant Earth control – especially crucial given communication delays of up to twenty minutes between Earth and Mars.

2. **Operational Precision Through Intelligent Systems:** Rather than brute-forcing solutions with expensive

---

[2] Wikipedia Contributors. 2019. "Mars Orbiter Mission." Wikipedia. Wikimedia Foundation. 27 October. https://tinyurl.com/3tw4d7t2.

[3] Pandey, Geeta. 2024. "Chandrayaan, Mangalyaan: Why It Costs India so Little to Reach the Moon and Mars." BBC, 4 November. https://tinyurl.com/mr2jf6xy.

redundancies, ISRO developed intelligent mission control systems that could integrate multiple data streams and execute precise operations with minimal resources.[4] These systems didn't just analyse – they actively controlled mission-critical functions.

3. **Frugal Execution Through Innovation:** Perhaps most impressively, ISRO reimagined the very process of interplanetary exploration. By executing smaller, more frequent course corrections rather than fewer large ones, by ingeniously using Earth's gravity for a fuel-saving slingshot manoeuvre and by designing multi-purpose scientific instruments, ISRO's systems achieved more with less.[5]

The societal impact of this approach extended far beyond scientific achievement. Mangalyaan carried scientific instruments that produced valuable data about Mars' atmosphere and surface features, but its equally important contribution was demonstrating that intelligent execution could overcome insurmountable resource constraints.

Mangalyaan's success also showcased the transformative potential of autonomous systems that could perceive,

---

[4] Joshi, Manjiri, and Sohil Sinha. 2024. "Beyond the Red Planet: How Mangalyaan Paved Way for Decade of Space Exploration." News18. 5 November. https://tinyurl.com/4kkx9n46.

[5] Thakore, Bijal. 2025. "The Space Review: To Mars with No Ambiguity of Purpose." Thespacereview.com. https://tinyurl.com/2u2bvbmt.

decide and adapt without human intervention across interplanetary distances. The spacecraft didn't merely follow instructions; it actively interpreted data and executed complex manoeuvres with minimal oversight, functioning effectively as an autonomous agent in space.

The DOES Framework: Autonomous Execution in the Age of Agentic AI

Just as Mangalyaan's autonomous capabilities marked a breakthrough in space exploration, artificial intelligence today is at a similar moment of transformation. While early AI technologies primarily consumed and processed information, today's agentic AI systems actively intervene in the world around them and make decisions on our behalf. Agentic systems leverage AI models to not only analyse data but also take actions independently. This leap from passive analysis to autonomous action marks a fundamental transformation in our technological capabilities – one that changes not just what machines can do, but how we approach problem-solving across every domain.

The DOES framework represents the pinnacle of AI literacy – where systems move beyond understanding (READS), creating (WRITES), calculating (ADDS) and strategizing (THINKS) to independently executing meaningful work with minimal human supervision. This final stage in the AI literacy journey unlocks the technology's most powerful potential yet: the ability to achieve complex goals through autonomous action in unpredictable environments.

What DOES Encompasses

- **Delegate to AI Agents:** Empower AI agents to handle routine tasks, manage schedules and execute pre-defined workflows, freeing up human resources for more strategic endeavours.

- **Orchestrate Complex Processes:** Utilize AI to monitor and manage complex operations, ensuring optimal performance, identifying potential issues and proactively recommending solutions.

- **Execute and Expedite:** Accelerate project execution and enhance operational efficiency by deploying AI agents to automate tasks, streamline processes and reduce turnaround times.

- **Support and Customer Success:** Deploy AI-powered chatbots and virtual assistants to provide instant support to customers, employees and other stakeholders. Enhance service levels and build stronger relationships.

In the pages that follow, we'll examine specific applications and methodologies for integrating each DOES component into your professional workflow.

Delegate to AI Agents

Think back to your last workday. How much time did you spend responding to routine emails, scheduling meetings, filing documents or managing other administrative tasks? For most leaders, these mundane but necessary activities consume 30–40 per cent of their working hours – precious time that could be devoted to strategic thinking, relationship building and creative problem-solving.

Across organizations, countless skilled professionals find themselves trapped in administrative quicksand – finance teams manually reconciling transactions, HR specialists processing standard requests, marketing professionals updating content across platforms. The collective opportunity cost is staggering, with organizations losing billions in potential innovation and growth while their most valuable minds handle work that doesn't fully leverage their capabilities.

That's where delegation to AI agents represents a profound shift in how we work. Unlike earlier waves of automation that required extensive programming for each specific task, today's AI agents can understand natural language instructions, adapt to changing contexts and execute complex workflows with minimal supervision. The barrier between "what I need done" and "getting it done" is disappearing, allowing people at every level to extend their impact without extending their hours.

But what does this delegation revolution actually look like in practice? Let's explore a real-world example:

Client Intelligence Challenge

At our executive AI bootcamp in March 2025, a Director at a leading IT services firm described a business challenge.

"We're managing a $12M digital transformation for a major broadcasting client, but I'm spending countless hours just trying to stay informed about their business," the executive explained. "My team manually tracks news from dozens of sources every few days – *this* takes away crucial cognitive bandwidth."

Just last month, they were blindsided during a steering committee meeting when the client referenced a strategic partnership that would impact their project roadmap – information their manual monitoring had completely missed. They'd also learned about an executive restructuring through a casual conversation rather than their formal intelligence channels.

"We need a way to stay ahead of these developments instead of constantly playing catch-up," the Director stated.

The issue was clear – fragmented monitoring and missed signals weren't allowing the team to stay on top of developments.

> ### AI Tool Recommendation
>
> **ChatGPT Tasks** is a productivity-focused feature within ChatGPT that allows users to schedule actions, reminders or updates such that they happen automatically. It acts as a digital assistant, working asynchronously to streamline workflows and ensure critical tasks are completed efficiently.
>
> Below are the key reasons why ChatGPT Tasks is the most suitable tool for this scenario:
> - **Automated Monitoring:** It can autonomously track and compile relevant news updates, sharing them with you at a scheduled time – ensuring the team stays informed without manual effort.
> - **Context-aware Outputs:** By leveraging user-provided context, it delivers tailored updates aligned with the business needs.
> - **Ease of Use:** The intuitive interface allows users to schedule recurring updates with minimal setup, ensuring consistency and reliability.

What Agentic Behaviours Does ChatGPT Tasks Show?

ChatGPT Tasks demonstrates agentic behaviours by autonomously executing predefined tasks based on user instructions. For instance, it can monitor specific sources for news updates, analyse the findings and deliver concise summaries without requiring constant human intervention. While it lacks true autonomy (e.g. independent decision-making), its ability to act within a predefined scope and adapt outputs based on contextual inputs reflects limited agentic properties.

Suggested Prompt

1. **Define the persona:**
   - You are a media-monitoring specialist with expertise in tracking corporate developments in the broadcasting industry.
2. **Set the context:**
   - I am a business leader managing a significant digital transformation project for a major broadcasting client. Staying updated on their latest news is crucial for aligning our strategies and avoiding surprises during steering committee meetings.
3. **Define the task:**
   - Monitor and compile the latest news and developments related to the broadcasting client, focusing on areas such as corporate announcements, financial results, strategic partnerships and industry trends. Summarize these updates in a concise format suitable for quick review.

4. **Define the desired output:**
   - **News Highlights:** A summary of the most recent and relevant news articles about the broadcasting client, including publication dates and sources.
   - **Key developments:** Brief descriptions of significant events or changes within the client's organization that could impact our project or strategic decisions.
5. **Define the boundaries:**
   - **Frequency:** Provide updates once a week on Monday at 8:00 a.m. IST.
   - **Sources:** Utilize reputable news outlets, industry reports and official press releases.
   - **Relevance:** Focus on news that directly pertains to the client's business activities.

Prompting Best Practices Followed

- **Clarity:** The prompt provides straightforward instructions with no ambiguity about what is expected from ChatGPT Tasks.
- **Context:** The scenario-specific details ensure that outputs are tailored to align with the user's business goals.
- **Precision:** Clear boundaries regarding frequency, sources and relevance guide ChatGPT Tasks to deliver focused results without unnecessary information.

How to Use the Tool

1. Open ChatGPT and log in to your account (Plus, Pro, or Team plan required).
2. Click on the model selection menu in the top left corner of the window.
3. Choose "ChatGPT-4o with Scheduled Tasks" from the dropdown menu.
4. In the chat interface, copy the suggested prompt, along with scheduling details (e.g. weekly updates every Monday at 8:00 a.m. IST).

How to Keep Your Data Safe

- **Avoid sharing sensitive information.** Do not input confidential details about your project or client into ChatGPT Tasks unless absolutely necessary.
- **Periodically review your scheduled tasks** to remove any that are no longer needed
- **Regularly audit task chat history.** Periodically review the task history and output logs to ensure no sensitive or unintended information has been processed or stored, helping to maintain data integrity and compliance.

Smart Ways to Review AI Output

- **Always check the AI-generated news summaries** and key developments against the original sources to confirm their accuracy.

- **Identify inconsistencies.** Look for any information that contradicts known facts or previous knowledge about the client. Flag and investigate any discrepancies.
- Confirm that **outputs align with your project's goals** and exclude unrelated information.

Outcome

By leveraging ChatGPT Tasks for automated media monitoring, the leader and his team were able to stay ahead of critical developments related to their client without relying on fragmented manual processes. Timely, scheduled updates ensured they were well informed about strategic partnerships, executive changes and other impactful events – helping them avoid surprises during steering committee meetings and enabling proactive alignment with their client's evolving priorities.

Orchestrate Complex Processes

Running any organization involves a ton of interconnected activity. Whether it's managing the flow of goods, coordinating a big project, handling market research or developing new products, there are always numerous processes with lots of moving parts and dependencies.

Traditionally, keeping these complex operations running smoothly has required significant human effort. Managers and teams spend countless hours tracking progress, monitoring metrics, deep-diving into research and reacting to problems as they arise. This can lead to delays, inefficiencies, less-than-ideal research outcomes and missed opportunities. Even with the best tools, it's easy to be overwhelmed by the sheer volume of information and the speed at which things change. For example, in market research, it can be a real challenge for analysts to synthesize information from various sources to produce clear, actionable insights. Similarly, in product development, it's often difficult for teams to effectively manage and analyse user feedback to drive product improvements.

AI agents are beginning to offer a new way to handle these complex processes. It's moving us beyond simply observing what's happening to optimizing workflows, and enhancing the efficiency and effectiveness of research.

So, how is this playing out in the real world? Let's explore another example.

Banking Strategy Clarity Gap

During our AI bootcamp session with financial services executives, a senior director from a top-tier bank shared a challenge he was facing. Tasked with presenting a comprehensive five-year technology strategy to the board, including positions on AI and quantum computing, the executive found himself at a crossroads. Despite having access to substantial market research and internal insights, he struggled to synthesize this information into a coherent, forward-looking vision.

"I have mountains of data and perspectives from various sources, but I'm finding it difficult to distill everything into a structured, defendable strategy," the executive explained. "With a board presentation approaching and the future direction of our technology investments at stake, I need to ensure my recommendations are both comprehensive and actionable."

The situation highlighted a common executive challenge: not just lack of information, but the increasing difficulty of transforming abundant insights into clear strategic direction when facing rapidly evolving technologies.

AI Tool Recommendation

ChatGPT Deep Research is an advanced AI research agent designed to perform comprehensive analysis on complex topics. It combines the reasoning capabilities of ChatGPT with enhanced research abilities, allowing it to synthesize information from multiple sources, evaluate complex scenarios and generate detailed reports with structured recommendations.

It is the most suitable tool for this banking strategy challenge because:

- It excels at synthesizing large volumes of complex information from multiple sources, which is perfect for distilling "mountains of data" into a coherent five-year technology strategy.

- Deep Research can perform deep analysis of industry-specific content, allowing it to provide nuanced insights about banking technology trends, AI applications and quantum computing impacts specific to financial services.
- It can generate comprehensive, structured outputs like the requested year-by-year strategy document with proper citations and references to official sources, which is essential for board-level presentations.

What Agentic Behaviours Does Deep Research Show?

Deep Research demonstrates several key agentic behaviours that make it suitable for complex strategic planning tasks. It autonomously breaks down multi-faceted problems into manageable components, actively searches for relevant information and synthesizes findings into cohesive outputs without continuous human intervention. When analysing banking strategy, it can independently identify knowledge gaps, determine what additional information is needed and structure its reasoning around financial metrics and industry-specific benchmarks. This agency allows it to move beyond simple question-answering towards becoming an active research partner that can reason through complex strategic challenges, prioritize information based on relevance and produce comprehensive actionable insights tailored to executive-level requirements.

Suggested Prompt

Context, Distribution and Objective
- I have a strategy presentation for my bank's board. I already have a robust set of slides for a 1-hour session. In addition to these slides, I need a comprehensive written report tailored for the Board of Directors. This report will be handed out in physical (hardcopy) form to board members, so it should be written and formatted for clear offline reading.

The main goals of this report are to:
- Outline the bank's overall 5-year strategy (year-by-year).
- Explain how AI can accelerate each aspect of that strategy (rather than being the entire focus).
- Begin with the bank's vision, mission and goals, as officially outlined and stated by leadership.

Key Requirements
- **Vision, Mission and Goals**
  - Begin the report by explicitly stating the bank's vision, mission and goals.
  - Cite official sources and quotes from prominent bank leaders wherever possible.

Five-Year Strategy (Year-by-Year)
- Develop a year-by-year roadmap for how the bank can achieve its business and operational objectives.
- In each year's plan, clearly reference back to the stated vision, mission and goals from the introduction.
- Include relevant numbers and metrics (e.g. market share targets, digital adoption rates, ROI estimates, customer engagement benchmarks) wherever appropriate to make the strategy more concrete and measurable.

AI as an Accelerator
- Demonstrate how AI can enhance or speed up the implementation of each year's initiatives, rather than framing it as a separate AI strategy.
- Provide examples, use cases and potential AI developments in the next 5 years.
- Where possible, quantify the impact of AI-driven initiatives (e.g. operational cost reduction percentages, customer retention rates, process automation gains).

Quantum Computing Considerations
- Include a section on the potential impact of quantum computing in financial services over the same 5-year period.
- Keep explanations concise and accessible for board members without deep technical expertise.

Mention possible metrics for evaluating quantum

advancements (e.g. speed improvements, cryptographic security benchmarks).
- **Accessibility and Audience**
  - Write for a board-level audience: clear, concise language with minimal tech jargon.
  - Since the report will be physically handed out, ensure readability with appropriate formatting (headings, spacing, clear typography, etc.).
- **Include Numbers and Metrics**
  - Wherever relevant, provide quantitative metrics that support the strategy, validate AI acceleration benefits or illustrate quantum computing potential.
  - Align such metrics with typical board-level KPIs (e.g. NPA reduction targets, market expansion goals, digital channel usage, etc.).
- **Proposed Report Structure**
  - Title Page
  - Table of Contents
  - Executive Summary (focus on the 5-year plan, how AI accelerates it and the big-picture outcomes)
  - Introduction: Bank's Vision, Mission and Goals
  - Bank's 5-Year Strategy (Year 1–5 breakdown)
  - AI Acceleration
  - Quantum Computing Impact
  - Conclusion and Recommendations
  - References

Prompting Best Practices Followed

1. **Specific task decomposition:** The prompt breaks down the complex strategy creation into clear components (vision, year-by-year strategy, AI acceleration, quantum computing) that Deep Research can tackle methodically.
2. **Clear output formatting instructions:** Detailed guidance on document structure, audience considerations and physical readability ensures the output meets executive presentation standards.
3. **Quantitative focus:** Explicit requests for metrics, benchmarks and quantifiable impacts guide Deep Research to produce actionable, measurable recommendations rather than generic suggestions.

Deep Research prompts differ from normal prompts because they operate at a higher level of abstraction, focusing on comprehensive research tasks rather than simple factual questions. They include extensive context-setting, clear objectives and detailed output requirements that enable the AI to perform multi-step reasoning across complex domains. These prompts essentially frame Deep Research as a strategic research partner rather than just a question-answering system.

How to Use the Tool

1. **Gather your key materials and context:** Collect relevant documents, data points and strategic objectives before crafting your prompt.
2. **Create a detailed, structured prompt:** Include clear context, objectives and specific requirements about the type of output you need.
3. **Submit and await initial response:** Go to https://chatgpt.com/. Select "New chat". Paste the prompt in the text-box. Select "Deep Research" and initiate the process. The process will take several minutes to complete.
4. **Review and refine with follow-up questions:** Analyse the output and use follow-up prompts to request clarification, additional detail or adjustments to specific sections.
5. **Export and format the final deliverable:** Once satisfied with the content, export the document and make any final formatting adjustments needed for your board presentation.

How to Keep Your Data Safe

- **Limit sensitive information sharing:** Only include necessary institutional data in your prompts; avoid proprietary financial figures, customer data or confidential strategic initiatives.
- **Use anonymized examples:** When providing context about your banking situation, use general descriptions

or anonymized examples rather than specific identifying details.
- **Set up data retention policies:** Ensure that any outputs generated by ChatGPT Deep Research are stored securely, and deleted when no longer needed. Implement data retention guidelines to minimize the risk of sensitive information lingering in storage unnecessarily.
- **Delete the chat conversation history** after the deep research task is done.

Smart Ways to Review AI Output

- **Cross-verify with official sources:** Ensure that the information and recommendations in the report are accurate by checking against the bank's official statements, industry reports and other reliable sources.
- **Identify and address inconsistencies:** Look for any discrepancies between the AI-generated content and known facts or established strategies. Correct or remove inaccurate information.
- **Validate quantitative projections:** Scrutinize any financial metrics, ROI estimates or operational efficiency gains to ensure they represent realistic projections for your specific banking context. Clarify vague recommendations. If the report includes ambiguous or generic suggestions, seek more detailed explanations or specific examples to make them actionable.

- **Assess practical implementation feasibility:** Evaluate whether the year-by-year roadmap and AI integration suggestions are technically feasible and compatible with your bank's infrastructure and capabilities.

Outcome

The senior banking director successfully leveraged Deep Research to transform their fragmented insights into a comprehensive five-year technology strategy. The structured report provided clear positioning on both AI and quantum computing applications in banking, with year-by-year implementation roadmaps tied directly to the bank's core mission and strategic objectives.

Execute and Expedite

You're in the thick of a high-stakes project launch, and the deadline is closing in fast. Your team is pulling late nights, but the pace is still dragging – manual data entry, endless approval loops and repetitive checks are eating up precious hours. Every delay feels like a lead weight, and you can see the frustration mounting as the finish line keeps slipping out of reach. You've got the talent and the vision, but the execution is getting bogged down in inefficiencies that no one saw coming.

This execution gap isn't just frustrating – it's existentially threatening in an era where markets reward speed and punish delay. Companies that move slowly find themselves perpetually playing catch-up, watching more agile competitors capture market opportunities and talent while they're still developing their response strategy.

By automating those tedious tasks and streamlining workflows, AI agents can cut through the clutter and speed things up – think faster processing, fewer bottlenecks and projects that hit their marks on time. These are agents that help you work smarter rather than harder, turning delays into deliverables with efficiency you didn't think was possible.

What does this acceleration actually look like in practice? Time to explore another real-world example.

The Developer's Context-Switching Dilemma

At an AI bootcamp with a renewable energy company in February 2025, we came across a scenario that shouldn't be necessary, yet has become an accepted part of developers' lives. Software developers were implementing a critical control system for a new renewable substation. The lead engineer was deep in coding the failsafe protocols when suddenly, they needed to find GitHub libraries that automate CI/CD pipelines.

As they reluctantly broke deep focus to search for the information, the engineer sighed while opening multiple browser tabs. "Every time I need to check documentation,

I lose 15–20 minutes of productive coding time," they explained during the sprint retrospective. "Last week, I was implementing a critical component and had to repeatedly switch between coding and searching through technical specifications, compliance requirements and legacy system documentation. What should have been a 4-hour task stretched into a full day." The team calculated that across six developers, they were losing approximately 30 hours weekly to context-switching and searching for information.

AI Tool Recommendation

When it comes to addressing the challenge of developer context-switching, **Proxy by Convergence.ai** is a suitable solution. Proxy by Convergence.ai is an AI agent designed to autonomously navigate the web, perform tasks and learn from interactions to enhance its capabilities over time. It operates by interacting with web browsers to execute tasks such as searching for information, automating workflows and retrieving data, thereby reducing the need for manual browsing and minimizing context-switching for developers.

Here are three key reasons why Proxy is particularly suited for this scenario:

- **Autonomous Web Interaction:** Proxy can independently perform web-based tasks, such as

searching for GitHub libraries that automate CI/CD pipelines, reducing the need for developers to manually search and switch contexts.
- **Continuous Learning and Adaptation:** Proxy employs Large Meta Learning Models (LMLMs) that enable it to learn new tasks and workflows over time, adapting to the specific needs of the user and improving its assistance capabilities.
- **Reduction of Cognitive Load:** By handling repetitive and time-consuming tasks, Proxy allows developers to maintain focus on complex coding activities, thereby enhancing productivity and reducing the cognitive load associated with context-switching.

What Agentic Behaviours Does Proxy Show?

Proxy exhibits agentic behaviours by actively performing tasks rather than passively generating text-based responses. It navigates websites, clicks buttons, fills forms and retrieves data as if a human were interacting with the interface. This ability to execute actions autonomously positions Proxy as an active participant in digital workflows.

Suggested Prompt

Act as a web assistant. Search GitHub for libraries that automate CI/CD pipelines. Provide a table summarizing supported platforms, latest updates, user ratings and key features. Ensure the information is accurate and up to date.

Prompting Best Practices Followed

1. **Specificity:** The prompt clearly specifies the task (searching GitHub libraries) and desired output format.
2. **Role Definition:** Using "Act as a web assistant" guides Proxy to behave in a targeted manner, ensuring relevant results.
3. **Output Customization:** Requesting structured results in a table format enhances usability and clarity.

How to Use the Tool

1. Visit https://proxy.convergence.ai/.
2. Enter the suggested prompt.
3. Initiate the browsing process by clicking the "Start" button.
4. Continue with your coding tasks while Proxy autonomously gathers the requested information.
5. After completion, review the AI-generated results on the Proxy platform.

How to Keep Your Data Safe

- **Understand how your data is handled.** Review Convergence.ai's privacy policy to know how Proxy manages and stores data.

- **Avoid entering proprietary code snippets** or internal system architecture details in your prompts
- **Minimize data exposure.** When assigning tasks to Proxy, ensure that no sensitive or confidential information is involved unless absolutely necessary and properly secured.

Smart Ways to Review AI Output

- **Cross-verify with original sources:** Confirm the accuracy of the library information by checking the official GitHub pages or documentation.
- **Check for inconsistencies:** Look for any outdated or incorrect data in the summary, such as wrong version numbers or misstated features.
- **Ensure relevance to your context:** Verify that the listed libraries meet your specific requirements, such as compatibility with your development environment or project needs.
- **Clarify any ambiguities:** If the summary contains unclear terms or lacks detail, seek additional information to fully understand the capabilities of each library.

Outcome

In this scenario, Proxy automated the search for CI/CD libraries on GitHub, compiling essential information into a structured format while allowing engineers to remain focused on their primary responsibilities. The development team was able to reduce distractions and minimize time lost to context-switching. Proxy's autonomous information retrieval allowed developers to maintain focus on critical coding tasks, enhancing productivity and reducing project timelines.

Support and Customer Success

Let's talk about the people on the front lines – the customer service reps, the help desk folks, the support teams. They're the ones interacting with your customers and employees every single day. Those interactions are absolutely key for building strong relationships, making sure people are happy and keeping them loyal. Customer expectations continue to rise, with majority of consumers now expecting personalized interactions and demanding immediate responses when they reach out for support.

The traditional approach to meeting these expectations relied on expanding support teams and contact centres. But this model has reached its breaking point. Support volumes continue to grow exponentially while budgets remain constrained. Even exceptional support teams can only handle so many simultaneous inquiries, creating inevitable bottlenecks during peak periods.

This is where AI agents are transforming the service landscape. Unlike simple chatbots or automated response systems, today's AI agents can understand complex questions, personalize responses based on customer context, handle multiple languages seamlessly and resolve a growing percentage of inquiries without human intervention. They don't replace human support – they elevate it, handling routine matters so human agents can focus where their empathy, creativity and judgment add the most value.

So, how are organizations using AI agents to really transform their support? Let's take a look our own example of leveraging AI agents for supporting our prospects.

Bridging the New Company Information Gap

In 2024, when we launched AI&Beyond – our organization focused on AI literacy for enterprises – we followed the standard approach of sending introductory emails with presentations and PDFs about our offerings to potential customers.

While prospects were familiar with our individual backgrounds, we found they still had many questions about our newly formed company – how our services worked, our methodology, case studies and pricing models. This created a stream of follow-up emails that slowed down the sales process. We realized there should be a better way to support these initial queries without the back and forth that delayed meaningful conversations about how we could actually help them.

> ### AI Tool Recommendation
>
> **ElevenLabs Conversational AI Agents** are highly suitable for bridging the information gap in the scenario described. Here are three key reasons:
> - **Natural Conversational Experience**: ElevenLabs integrates advanced speech recognition, text generation and voice synthesis, enabling seamless human-like interactions that answer client queries naturally and efficiently.
> - **Customization and Scalability**: The platform allows businesses to deploy voice agents tailored to their needs, with features like turn-taking and interruption handling, ensuring adaptability across diverse client interactions.
> - **Efficiency and Cost-effectiveness**: By automating responses to common queries, ElevenLabs reduces follow-up emails and speeds up the sales process, saving time and operational costs.

What Agentic Behaviours Does ElevenLabs Conversational AI Agents Show?

ElevenLabs Conversational AI Agents exhibit agentic behaviours by interpreting user intent, dynamically engaging in conversations and responding appropriately based on pre-defined goals. For instance, they can pause when interrupted or adapt their tone and depth of explanation depending on the user's expertise level, showcasing both autonomy and contextual understanding.

Suggested Prompt

The Conversational AI Agent is available as a link to the recipient. The recipient can invoke the link and ask the questions such as:
- "What services does AI&Beyond offer?"
- "How does AI&Beyond support enterprises in healthcare?"
- "What case studies demonstrate your success?"
- "Can you explain your pricing models?"

How to Set up the ElevenLabs Conversational AI Agent

1. **Sign Up:** Create an account on ElevenLabs' platform: https://elevenlabs.io/app/conversational-ai/agents.
2. **Configure Agent Settings:** Customize voice profiles, initial messages and system prompts based on company needs.
3. **Integrate Knowledge Base:** Train the agent using company documentation for accurate responses.
4. **Test Interactions:** Use the platform's testing tools to refine conversational flow.

5. **Deploy:** Launch the agent across web or telephony channels for client use.

How to Keep Your Data Safe

- **Upload only publicly available content** rather than internal strategy documents to the knowledge base.
- **Regularly audit your agent's knowledge base** and remove outdated information to prevent sharing inaccurate details about your offerings.
- **Ensure secure access.** Enable authentication for your ElevenLabs account and treat agent IDs as confidential to prevent unauthorized access.

Smart Ways to Review AI Output

- **Regularly sample conversations** and check the AI's responses against accurate information sources or company documentation to ensure correctness.
- **Identify and correct inconsistencies.** Flag any responses that provide incorrect or outdated information and update the agent's knowledge base accordingly.
- **Evaluate contextual appropriateness.** Ensure that the AI's responses are suitable for the specific customer queries and reflect the company's tone and policies.
- If the AI provides unclear or generic answers, **refine the prompts or training data to encourage more precise and helpful responses.**

Outcome

By deploying ElevenLabs Conversational AI Agents, we were able to streamline the early part of customer onboarding process by addressing common queries instantly through natural voice interactions. This reduced follow-up emails, accelerated meaningful conversations about services and enhanced customer satisfaction – all while maintaining cost efficiency and scalability in operations.

A Continuation

"AI is whatever hasn't been done yet."
— LARRY TESLER

Most books end with a conclusion; this continues from here on.

The ten chapters that you've hopefully read through and applied in your life mark the beginning of your AI journey. The first four chapters of the book should have made you much more informed about the most powerful technology of our generation. The book's READS-to-DOES methodology, detailed in Chapters 6–10, would definitely have made you AI-literate and equipped you to use GenAI, substantially increasing your productivity, efficiency and creativity.

However, the last two years have seen AI move at the speed of thought, an almost superhuman pace, that no one has seen in technology before. Every new week, sometimes every new day, brings a new tool or feature that takes one's breath away, and makes a few earlier ones redundant. As the saying goes, "There are decades where nothing happens; and there are weeks where decades happen." This is as true for politics as it is for how fast AI and GenAI are developing, where weeks, and even days, seem like decades.

While a lot of tools and agents we have used and demonstrated in the book are fundamental and will be in use for a long while, you can expect fresh upgrades, releases and next generations to pop up very quickly. For example, ChatGPT, which started this revolution on 30 November 2022, was built on GPT-3.5. In less than three years since, it has become quaint and antiquated. At the time of writing this book, we have had eleven fundamental updates on just this model itself, as I describe below:

1. **GPT-3 (November 2022):** The first version of ChatGPT, powered by GPT-3.5, introduced improved language comprehension and text generation capabilities compared to GPT-3.

2. **GPT-3.5 Turbo (2023):** An enhanced version of GPT-3.5 with better accuracy and reduced latency, available for free and through API access.

3. **GPT-4 (March 2023):** Introduced with the ChatGPT Plus subscription, this model offered significant advancements in reasoning, safety and multimodal capabilities (e.g. processing images).

4. **GPT-4o (May 2024):** A multimodal model capable of processing and generating text, images, audio and video in real time. It was faster, more efficient and included advanced multilingual capabilities.

A Continuation

5. **GPT-4o Mini (July 2024):** A smaller and more cost-effective version of GPT-4o within ChatGPT's free tier that replaced GPT-3.5.

6. **o1-preview (September 2024):** A pre-release version of OpenAI's "o1" model with enhanced reasoning capabilities.

7. **o1-mini (September 2024):** A smaller and faster variant of the o1-preview model.

8. **o1 (December 2024):** The full release of the o1 model, offering better reasoning and performance compared to earlier versions.

9. **o1 Pro Mode (December 2024):** An upgraded version of o1 with higher computational power, available to ChatGPT Pro subscribers.

10. **o3-mini (January 2025):** A successor to o1-mini with further improvements in speed and efficiency.

11. **o3-mini-high (January 2025):** A variant of o3-mini designed for more complex reasoning tasks.

12. **GPT-4.5 (February 2025):** A particularly large model described as OpenAI's "last non-chain-of-thought model", emphasizing advanced reasoning and comprehension capabilities.

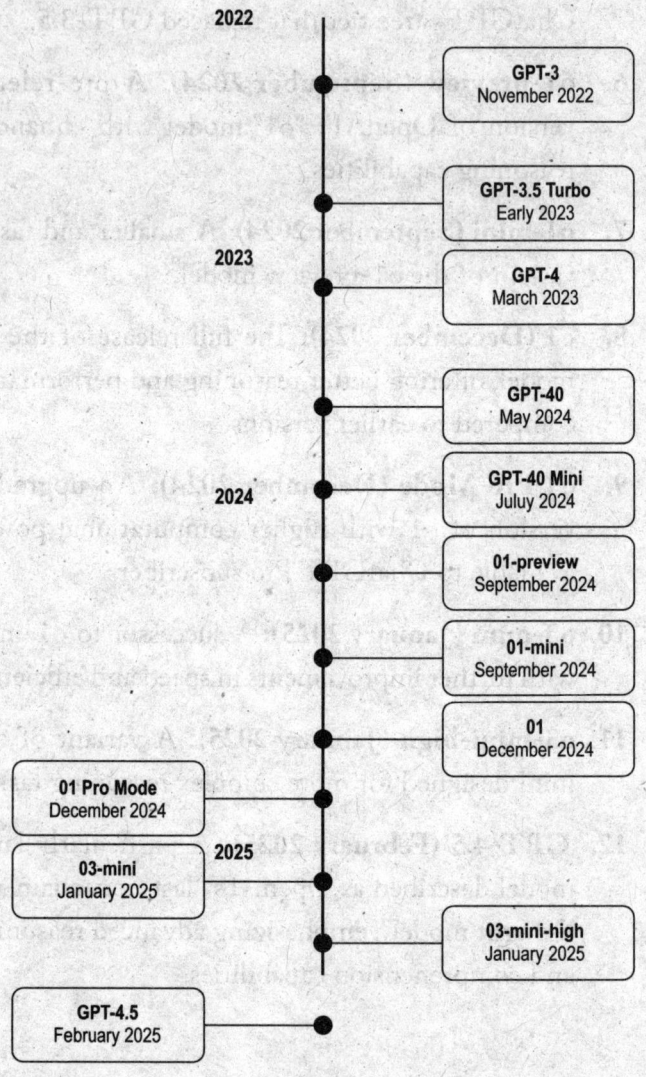

A Continuation

The list above does not even take into account some of the features of ChatGPT, which we have used in the book, like Tasks, Canvas, Images, Deep Research, Projects, etc., or even other parallel products launched by them like Sora and DALL-E 2. What this also does not capture is how each of these were introduced as paid models, sometimes at $200 per month, and swiftly either dropped down to $20 a month, or became completely free.

As we know, there are other players like OpenAI, which are putting out new AI models and products at dazzling speed. Google with the Gemini Series; Microsoft with Copilot, Phi and Orca; Anthropic with its Claude family; Meta with the LlaMA brood; the French company Mistral with Mixtral; and the Chinese churning out high quality models like DeepSeek, Ernie and Qwen. Thousands of innovative startups are building great applications on top of the models, some of which we have seen like Gamma.app, Whimsical.ai, Smallest.ai and Eleven Labs.

Thus, becoming AI-literate through this book is just your first very important step. It has equipped you with the understanding of the "language" of GenAI, the fundamental tools and skills that working with it involves and, hopefully, made you as excited and awestruck by it as we, the authors, are.

The next steps are to keep up with it. To help you do that, we will continue the AI literacy effort through our website **www.ailiteracybook.com**. It is structured the same way the book is. The home page offers some of the background to AI literacy, while the rest of the pages follow the READS-to-DOES framework. The authors will continue to add important new developments and tools to each of these five fundamental steps as they develop.

As we go forward, we will also preview new launches and developments in this website, and also through www.aiandbeyond.ai. We also encourage you to visit one of the authors' writings on AI on www.jaspreetbindra.com, where you can learn about the latest opinions and impact of this technology. Our goal is to build a community of like-minded people like you, dear readers, through this website, so that we can all not only learn from the book and the website, but from each other too.

We are also building an AI agent for this book, which can serve as your personal AI literacy assistant – stay tuned for an announcement on our website!

As you turn the final page, know that this isn't goodbye. We'd love to stay connected – come visit us at www.ailiteracybook.com. See you there, soon.

Acknowledgements

I woke up early on 1 December 2022 and, as is my wont, looked at my phone bleary-eyed. Something called ChatGPT had been launched by OpenAI, a company I'd been tracking for some time, as it appeared to be delivering minor miracles for hundreds of deliriously happy early users. I jumped out of bed, booted my laptop, and was lost to ChatGPT for the next few hours, becoming one more statistic in the million users it garnered that week – the fastest tech product rollout in history.

I was already deeply immersed in the world of tech and AI – in fact, I was at the University of Cambridge to pursue my (second late-life) Master's, this time in AI and Ethics – I knew that the world had irrevocably changed. The tectonic plates below humanity had shifted decisively and nothing was going to be the same again.

For the next 30 days, I dropped everything else I was doing, and walked into the weeds of Large Language Models, transformers and prompts even as the world around me descended into a generative AI-fuelled orgy of having ChatGPT spinning out delightful poems and character impersonations.

Since then, everything I have done in my life has been around AI in general, and generative AI in particular. I embarked on a new career in writing, speaking, teaching, advising and wondering about AI.

Thus, the first 'person' I must thank is ChatGPT, the ancestor of all GPT models that exist today, and its creators at OpenAI – names that have become legendary now. My thanks also to its numerous siblings who have been born since – Claude, Gemini, CoPilot, LlaMA, DeepSeek, Sarvam, and so many others. The children that these models have created, chiefly Perplexity, Eleven, Smallest, Gamma, Napkin, Canva.ai and so many others, have transformed my life and made me at least 2x more efficient, productive and creative. The book would have taken four times the time if they were not around.

Acknowledgements

Moving to humans, I must begin by thanking my co-founder at AI&Beyond, Anuj Magazine, who gamely went ahead with another crazy idea of mine and agreed to co-author this book with me.

The wonderful clients I work with, chief among them ThoughtWorks and CGI especially, for agreeing to become willing subjects of our AI experiments. The hundreds of organizations and their CEOs and CHROs, who invited me to share my wonder about AI. The many wonderful organizations and the inspirational leaders there that I have worked with – Tata Administrative Services, Microsoft, Mahindra Group. My professors at Cambridge – Stephen Cave, Henry Shevlin, Jonnie Penn, Maya Indira Ganesh, and my fellow students of the first guinea pig cohort at my Master's program. A big shoutout to *Mint*, the newspaper which patiently published more than 150 of my columns on AI and tech, and many other publications for readily accepting my regularly 'occasional' columns.

Teesta, my editor at Juggernaut Books, for swallowing her initial shock and accepting to publish this book at record speed, and Rachna Kalra, my friend, for pointing me towards her. Great, enduring friends – they know who they are, but none of whom knew I was writing this book on the side. They kept on feeding me the fib that any book I write will be the greatest ever, while simultaneously criticizing every tiny aspect of it.

My maternal aunt, Sheela Singh, has been a rock of support, and so are her sons. So are several members of my extended family, especially my big sister, Jasleen Kaur. My greatest thanks to my sister, Prerna Singh Bindra, a five-time author and current PhD student at Cambridge, for always believing in me, even at times when I didn't.

My final thanks are reserved for my parents, especially my late mother, Jatinder Bindra, to whom this book is dedicated. More than anything else, they instilled in me a love for reading and for books and encouraged me to be curious. Without her influence, I would've left a lot of books unread, and this one would certainly never have been written.

Jaspreet Bindra

Acknowledgements

Jaspreet Bindra: When Jaspreet came up with the idea of this book, I had only one thought, inspired by that popular quote: "When you are offered a seat on a rocket ship, you don't ask which seat. You just get on." And what a journey it has been.

Jaspreet's innovative spirit and exemplary work ethic have been the very foundation of this book. Given how fast AI is evolving, this book was always about keeping pace with the dramatic changes unfolding in the field, a race against time where the finish line kept moving further away each day.

AI&Beyond's customers: Thank you so much for sharing such rich perspectives and conversations that added immense value to this book. Your willingness to experiment with AI and provide candid feedback shaped not just our trajectory as a company but the core insights of this manuscript. Your trust in our vision and partnership in navigating this technological frontier has been both humbling and inspiring.

Our readers: Thank you for choosing this book! I truly hope it inspires and empowers you on your journey. In a world where AI literacy has become as fundamental as digital literacy was a decade ago, my deepest wish is that these pages provide you with the understanding and confidence to navigate this new reality that's emerging – not as passive observers, but as empowered participants shaping how these technologies integrate into our lives.

My family: My father, Tej Magazine, for instilling in me a strong work ethic, and my father-in-law, Surinder Wali, for always believing in me. And to my moms, the late Raj Magazine and the late Usha Wali – your memories light my path. I know you would have been proud. To Shweta, my partner and lifeline, and to Anusheel, my joy and reason for striving to be better – the countless times you listened to my excited ramblings about new discoveries or breakthroughs in AI shaped this work in ways you might never realize.

My friends: who endured my temporary disappearance from social life – thank you for understanding that this book demanded a singular focus.

Anuj Magazine

A Note on the Authors

Jaspreet Bindra is the CEO and Co-founder of AI&Beyond, a company that employs both humans and AI agents to build AI literacy in organizations. He is also the managing director of Tech Whisperer Ltd, UK. Previously, he served as regional director at Microsoft, a chief digital officer-equivalent executive at the Mahindra Group and was an officer of the Tata Administrative Services.

Jaspreet is a visiting faculty at Ashoka University and an expert at Singularity University. He contributes regularly to the *Economic Times*, was a long-time columnist for *Mint* and is the author of the bestselling book *The Tech Whisperer: On Digital Transformation and the Technologies that Enable It*, published by Penguin Random House India.

A biological human being, Jaspreet is an engineer and MBA, and holds a Master's in AI Ethics and Society from the University of Cambridge.

More at www.jaspreetbindra.com and www.ailiteracybook.com.

Anuj Magazine is Co-founder and CTO of AI&Beyond, and a tech innovator with 16 US patents. With a distinguished portfolio career focused on AI and cybersecurity, he has held leadership roles across organizations ranging from the Fortune 1 company Walmart to several Fortune 500 companies such as Citrix, McAfee and Quark. Anuj also serves as an advisor to startups in the cybersecurity and fitness/well-being sectors. He is the author of *What's Your Human Edge: 53 Timeless Ideas for Thriving in the Age of AI*.

For more insights from the authors, visit www.ailiteracybook.com.